Preparing for the Psychology AP* Exam

with

Zimbardo, Johnson, Weber, and Gruber

Psychology

AP* Edition

prepared by

Diane Finley
Prince George's Community College

Geraldine Acquard
Walter Johnson High School

PEARSON

Boston   New York   San Francisco
Mexico City   Montreal   Toronto   London   Madrid   Munich   Paris
Hong Kong   Singapore   Tokyo   Cape Town   Sydney

ISBN 13:   978-0-13-173077-9
ISBN 10:   0-13-173077-0

Printed in the United States of America

10 9 8 7 6 5 4 3 2 1   10 09 08 07 06

Preface

This guide is intended to help you as you prepare for the AP Psychology exam. The exam is an important milestone in your secondary education. Scoring well means you will have more options in college.

In this guide you will find:

❖ **A guide to the AP Psychology Exam**
   This section explains a bit about the AP Psychology exam. It also contains tips for studying and preparing for the exam.

❖ **Chapter Summaries**
   These highlight the major concepts and terms that you should know as you prepare for the exam.

❖ **Practice Quizzes**
   These questions are constructed to be similar to those you will find on the AP Psychology exam.

❖ **Answers to the Quizzes**
   The answers are included to help you as you prepare for the exams.

This guide was written by a college professor who was a Reader for the AP Psychology exam for thirteen years and a high school psychology teacher who has taught AP Psychology for fourteen years.

We hope you will read all of this material as well as your textbook as you prepare for the exam. We have attempted to provide you with some tools to help you as prepare for the exam. Using the tools is up to you. Good luck!

Dr. Diane Finley, Prince George's Community College, Largo MD
Ms. Geraldine Acquard, Walter Johnson High School, Bethesda MD

Acknowledgements

Working on this project was not done in solitude.
Specifically we would like to thank:

- The authors of this text: Philip Zimbardo, Robert Johnson, Ann Weber, and Craig Gruber, for writing a textbook that students find interesting and readable. We are grateful to have had a part in preparing this resource for AP students.

- Our editor, Liz DiMenno, whose answers to our questions have made this process more enjoyable and doable.

- Our families, especially Charlie, Matt, Danny, and Brian Acquard, and Sallye Finley, for their patience and support as we worked to prepare this resource on schedule.

TABLE OF CONTENTS

What is the Advanced Placement (AP) Psychology exam?

Advanced Placement Psychology is one of the twenty subject areas in which the College Board offers courses and exams. The courses are taught at the college-level and are designed for secondary school students who are highly motivated. Most college and universities in the United States as well as in over thirty countries grant credit or advanced standing to students who do well on the Advanced Placement (AP) exams.

The AP Psychology course is equivalent to the Introduction to Psychology or General Psychology course given in most colleges and universities. This course is designed to introduce students to the scientific study of human behavior and of mental processes. The research methodology used by psychologists is examined in detail as are the subfields of psychology. AP courses cover the same material and focus on the scientific aspects of the discipline.

Why should a student take an AP Psychology course?

Why take an AP Psychology course? There are many benefits to completing AP Psychology. It is possible to receive college credit for the introductory psychology course. Introduction to Psychology often meets general education requirements. It is also the prerequisite for most upper-level psychology courses. Successfully completing the AP exam and receiving course credit allows a student to go directly into these upper-level courses. It also may allow a student to fulfill a general education requirement, freeing up credits to be explored in other disciplines. Introduction to Psychology is also required for many majors including nursing, education and physical therapy. Earning credit through the AP exam helps fulfill that requirement. College admission officers look favorably at AP credit on a high school transcript.

There are many other benefits to completing AP Psychology. The course helps you to develop research skills which can be used in many disciplines. It leads to improved writing skills. The course gives students a deeper understanding of human behavior. Finally, the course helps to develop critical thinking skills.

What is the exam like?

AP exams are administered at schools that participate in the AP program. The exam consists of two sections: multiple choice and free response. The multiple choice section consists of 100 questions. Students are given seventy minutes to complete this section. Questions come from the various topics taught in the AP Psychology course. The questions become progressively more difficult. The content breakdown of the questions closely follows the percentages listed in the multiple choice question table.

The multiple choice questions occur in the following percentages:

2-4%	history
6-8%	methods and approaches
8-10%	biological bases of behavior
7-9%	sensation and perception
2-4%	states of consciousness
7-9%	learning
8-10%	cognition
7-9%	motivation and emotion
7-9%	developmental psychology
6-8%	personality
5-7%	testing and individual differences
7-9%	abnormal psychology
5-7%	treatment of psychological disorders
7-9%	social psychology

There are two free-response questions. Students have fifty minutes to answer both questions. These questions require students to answer in essay format and to make connections between the various domains of the discipline. Questions require students to use content from more than one chapter in order to earn full points. Students may be asked to design a research study within given parameters. They may be asked to explain a particular concept from several different theoretical perspectives. Questions change each year. They are pre-tested with college populations to assure comparability.

How is the exam scored?

The multiple choice questions account for two-thirds of the total score. This section is machine scored. When completing the multiple choice questions, students should not guess haphazardly because there is a correction factor in the scoring. One-fourth of the number of questions answered incorrectly is subtracted from the multiple choice score. If one (or more) options can be eliminated as incorrect, it is usually good to choose from the remaining answers.

The two free response questions account for one-third of the score. Each is worth one-sixth of the total score. These questions are scored by college professors and high school AP psychology teachers using a rubric developed by a team of expert teachers. Reliability of this scoring is very high.

Students earn scores of 1 to 5. The raw scores are converted to this scale of 1 to 5. AP score cutoffs are not set as are traditional grade cutoffs. The scores are scaled and change from year to year depending on how students taking the exam do.

How can the Zimbardo, Johnson, Weber, and Gruber text help students be successful on the AP exam?

The Zimbardo, Johnson, Weber, and Gruber text has many built-in study aids that can help when studying for the AP exam. One of the authors, Craig Gruber, has taught AP Psychology for many years. He is also a Faculty Consultant who read (scored) the AP exam for over ten years. His expertise helped shape this text so that students can achieve maximum success on the exam.

The chapter content and the organization closely follow that of the outline developed by the College Board. The outline is included in the textbook. The "Psychology in Your Life" sections aid in the development of critical thinking. If written as essays, they would help students with writing skills.

"Check Your Understanding" and "Review Tests" help students assess their knowledge as they go through the material. These elements also serve as review for the exam. "Connection Arrows" throughout the chapters make explicit links between concepts found across chapters. This is critical preparation for the free response questions. Finally, an "AP Review" section at the end of each chapter highlights pertinent vocabulary and concepts. It also includes sample essay questions.

Suggested Study Plan and Schedules

The AP exam is administered in early May. That means that teachers and student have about eight months or thirty-two weeks to prepare for the exam. Ideally the class should finish covering the text by the end of April. That leaves the first two weeks of May for intensive review although studying and review needs to begin in September, as soon as school begins. There are fourteen chapters in this text. That means that classes can spend about two weeks on each chapter and still leave room for vacation weeks.

It is important to begin studying for the AP exam as soon as you begin reading the text. Make lists of the concepts and terms. Write definitions for each in your own words. Putting them on flashcards is a good technique. It is important to know the definitions of terms but students should also be able to apply them correctly, understand their fine distinction, and link them to related terms. It is also important to be able to identify the psychologist who originated the terms and the theory or perspective most closely associated with the terms. Students must be careful when learning terms that seem similar but actually have important differences. Some of those term pairs are: negative reinforcement/punishment, heritability/inherited, random sample/assignment, independent/dependent variable, habituation/sensory adaptation, and generalization/generalizability.

Make detailed outlines that follow the College Board content outlines. Be sure to do all of the practice tests. Go over the answers and be sure you understand why the answers are correct or not. Be sure to go over each test and examine answers in detail.

Go back to previous chapters at least once a month. As the number of chapters completed grows, schedule one day each week to review a chapter. Remember that repetition helps memory.

Create your own practice questions. Trade with friends and then go over the answers. Get the previous tests from the College Board and study them. Try taking the previous tests under the same conditions as the AP exam. During the two weeks before the exam, be sure to review each chapter at least two times.

General Exam Tips

1. Relax before the exam. Get a good night's sleep and try to clear your mind of distracting thoughts.

2. Eat something that will provide you with energy before the exam. You will think more clearly, and you will not be distracted by hunger pangs.

3. Plan your study time effectively. Your text has a suggested study schedule that guides your preparation for the exam. Cramming is not advised, but a last minute review of a few difficult terms may be helpful.

4. The exam is two hours long and divided into two parts. A multiple-choice part has 100 questions and then there is a short break before you have to answer two free response questions. Manage your time throughout the exam.

Tips for Success on the Multiple Choice Questions

1. The first few questions are usually less challenging than later questions. This provides you with some comfort as you progress through the exam. The questions generally become more challenging as the exam progresses.

2. A good exam strategy is to go through all of the multiple-choice questions and answer all those questions you know as quickly as you can, keeping track of any questions about which you are uncertain. You should have enough time to go back and complete the noted questions.

3. Be sure to read the entire question through before answering. Identify the key words in the "stem" or question part. Try to eliminate some of the options. If you cannot eliminate any of the options and do not know what the question is asking, skip it. There are deductions for wrong answers so you don't want to wildly guess. Do not spend a lot of time on any one question. There are 100 questions on the exam.

REMEMBER YOU HAVE ABOUT 42 SECONDS PER QUESTION.

4. Do not expect to know the answers to every question on the AP exam. You should not stress about getting 100 percent on the AP exam. The questions come from a variety of sources and

are not based on your text alone. The exam is very vocabulary-driven. Your best preparation is a vocabulary card with each term/name, its definition, an example or application of the term, and two association words.

An example of this is the term *id*. Your vocabulary card might read: *id- the primitive, unconscious portion of personality that houses basic drives and repressed memories (definition). It functions like a child that wants gratification <u>right now (example)</u>, Freud, impulsive (association words).* The association words help you if you have trouble understanding the question posed in the exam.

5. It is okay to skip a couple of questions on the Multiple Choice section. If you <u>truly</u> have no idea what the answer would be, then leave it blank. The conventional wisdom from some AP teachers is to eliminate at least half of the options, if you can, and then make a good choice. Again, search for your association words in the options presented to you.

Tips for Success on the Free Response Questions

1. Read the question carefully. Answer the question asked. Do not just talk about the general topic. Be specific about psychological theories and constructs. Cite evidence and use examples to illustrate the answer if the question calls for examples. Use psychological terms correctly. Do not include irrelevant, peripheral issues.

2. Try to estimate the number of points for each question and aim to make that many points in your response. Often there are parts to the question that are clues to the number of points.

   See the rubrics of previous exams for the best examples. They clearly indicate the guidelines of how the readers score points. They are available on-line. Generally, the free-response rubric awards one point for the definition and one point for application to the question. Each free-response question is generally comprehensive, taking vocabulary from many different topics covered throughout the year.

3. You must write the free response answer in extended paragraph form. DO NOT OUTLINE, BULLET, or NUMBER in your response. Write legibly, even if it means you have to print. The readers can only correct what they can read.

   Underline the term you are answering so the readers can identify what part of the question you are answering. Skip a line in between each term if it makes your response easier to read. You will not lose points for skipping a line in between each term. It is very important that the reader knows what part of the question you are addressing in your response. Make sure your response is clear and answers the question posed.

   You will not be marked on your English proficiency, so do not spend time polishing your response. Do not restate the question in the introductory paragraph or craft a closing paragraph that would be appropriate for an English class essay. Simple answer the question asked in complete sentences.

4. Be sure to include examples related to the topic, if is appropriate to the question posed. This demonstrates that you understand the question and can apply proper psychological terminology in an appropriate way. Remember that you are allotted about twenty-five minutes for completion of each free response question. Keep track of your time.

5. If you are confused or truly do not know the answer, write about something related to the question. Always include definitions, as you might be awarded some points. Only use this technique if absolutely did not understand the question. Include examples from class, including videos and activities. DO NOT leave any free-response question blank!

6. If you remember something related to Question #1 while answering Question #2, go back and insert your additional information. If you have run out of room on Question #1 and did not leave enough room for your additional information, give the reader specific instructions about where you are placing this additional information. Give clear instructions which say something like "the rest of this answer follows Question #2." Because readers score only one question, they may not look at the back of the booklet for additional information.

Chapter One – Introduction to and History of Psychology

What Is Psychology-and What Is It Not?

Core Concept - Psychology is a broad field with many specialties, but fundamentally, psychology is the scientific study of behavior and mental processes.

Psychology includes the study of *behaviors* (observable actions –like walking and speaking) and *mental processes* (internal processes that are indirectly observed-like thinking and feeling). The *science* of psychology is based on objective and verifiable methodology and study. The **empirical approach** is the standard for all psychological research. The empirical approach means that a study is conducted through careful observation and scientifically based research.

One goal of this course is to have the reader become a critical thinker. Critical thinkers can differentiate between psychology and **pseudopsychology.** Pseudopsychology is unscientific psychology that presents itself as scientific psychology.

One harmful effects of pseudopsychology include the **confirmation bias.** The confirmation bias is the tendency for humans to pay attention to events that confirm and support their beliefs, while they ignore evidence that does not support their beliefs. Other harmful effects of pseudopsychology include the potential for serious harm and potential fraud. Facilitated communication demonstrates how pseudopsychology has led to the use of invalid therapies for psychological disorders. Psychology students should develop critical thinking skills when reading reports about psychological issues.

Psychologists specialize in many different areas. Psychologists are not all therapists. Psychology is practiced in three different ways. **Experimental psychology** involves basic research on psychological processes. **Applied psychology** uses the knowledge developed by experimental psychologists to solve human problems. **Teaching psychology** involves teaching at the high school, college, or university level and may overlap with experimental psychology.

There are several applied psychology specialties. These specialties include industrial/organizational psychology, sport psychology, engineering psychology, school psychology, rehabilitation psychology, clinical psychology, and counseling psychology.

Psychiatry and psychology are different. **Psychiatry** is a medical specialty that involves the diagnosis and treatment of mental disorders. A psychiatrist earns an M.D. degree while a psychologist earns either a Ph.D. or a Psy.D.

What Are Psychology's Historical Roots?

Core Concept - Modern psychology developed from several conflicting traditions, including structuralism, functionalism, Gestalt psychology, behaviorism, and psychoanalysis.

Human behavior and mental processes have been explored throughout history and across cultures. The contemporary view of psychology has evolved from the ideas of the earliest philosophers.

Advances in natural sciences like biology and chemistry led to insights about human behavior. **Structuralism** is a historical school of psychology founded by **Wilhelm Wundt** in 1879. It focused on the structures that make up mind and thought, rather than what the mind could do (consciousness). In his lab in Leipzig, Germany, Wundt used a technique called **introspection.** Introspection is the process of reporting one's conscious mental experiences.

Functionalism is a historical school of psychology founded by **William James** who believed that mental processes could best be understood in terms of their adaptive purpose and function. **Gestalt psychology** is a historical school of psychology that tried to understand how the brain works by studying perceptions and perceptual learning. Gestalt psychologists including **Max Wertheimer** and **Wolfgang Kohler** believed that percepts consist of meaningful wholes (Gestalts).

Behaviorism is a historical school of psychology, led by **John B. Watson** that attempted to make psychology an objective science focused only on behavior—excluding all mental processes. **Psychoanalysis** is an approach to psychology based on **Sigmund Freud**'s beliefs that emphasized unconscious processes. This term refers to Freud's psychoanalytic theory and his psychoanalytic treatment method. An introspective look at the Necker Cube illustrates that humans do not sense the world as it really is, but perceive the world by adding personal interpretations of experiences.

What Are the Perspectives Psychologists Use Today?

Core Concept - There are nine main perspectives that characterize modern psychology: the biological, developmental, cognitive, psychodynamic, humanistic, behavioral, sociocultural, evolutionary/sociobiological, and trait views.

The **biological perspective** searches for the causes of behavior in heredity (genetics), the brain, nervous system, and endocrine (hormone) system. Biological psychology along with biology, neurology, and other disciplines interested in brain processes are collectively referred to as **neuroscience. Evolutionary psychology** draws from the work of **Charles Darwin** and explains behavior and mental processes in terms of their genetic adaptations for survival and reproduction.

The **developmental perspective** explores changes that occur across the lifespan. Developmental psychologists explore the contributions of heredity and environment, of nature vs. nurture.

The **cognitive perspective** explains that our actions are influenced by the way we process information coming from our environment. The cognitive view emphasizes **cognitions**, which are mental processes such as learning, memory, perception, thinking, and information processing. An interdisciplinary field that studies the connections among mind, brain, and behavior is called **cognitive neuroscience**.

The **clinical view** emphasizes mental health and mental illness. The **psychodynamic perspective** states that we are motivated primarily by the energy of irrational desires that are generated in our unconscious minds. This viewpoint emphasizes the understanding of mental disorders in terms of unconscious needs, desires, memories, and conflicts.

The **humanistic perspective** emphasizes human ability, growth, potential, and free will. Led by **Abraham Maslow** and **Carl Rogers,** humanists emphasize free will, self-concept, and the importance of self-concept.

The **behavioral perspective** finds the source of our actions in our external environment, rather than in our inner mental processes or our biology. Rewards and punishments shape how we act.

The **sociocultural view** states that social influence is the focus of psychology. This view emphasizes the importance of social relations, social learning, and one's culture. **Culture** is a complex blend of language, beliefs, customs, values, and traditions developed by a group of people and shared with others in the same environment.

The **evolutionary/sociobiological perspective** looks at human behavior and mental processes as adaptive and hereditary. Behavior is determined by natural selection.

The **trait perspective** views behavior and personality as the products of enduring psychological characteristics. Individual differences result from differences in our underlying patterns of stable characteristics called **traits**. Behavior results from each person's unique combination of traits.

Modern psychology is very diverse and changing very rapidly. Women and ethnic minorities make up of a significant proportion of psychological professionals. Individuals interested in pursuing a career in psychology should realize that an advanced degree beyond the bachelor's degree is required for most psychological career options.

Sample Multiple Choice

1. According to your text, the best definition of psychology is _____.
   A. the understanding of unconscious processes
   B. the study of the human mind
   C. the scientific study of human behaviors
   D. the exploration of personality traits
   E. the scientific study of behavior and mental processes

2. The empirical approach to psychological research is best reflected in which of the following statements?
   A. There are many specialties within the field of psychology.
   B. A psychological study is conducted through careful observation and scientifically-based research.
   C. Observable actions, like speaking and walking, are more valuable to research than mental processes like thinking and feeling.
   D. People can interpret results of psychological studies in many different ways.
   E. Most psychological studies are the result of the confirmation bias.

3. Dr. Smith works at a research facility where her team is trying to establish a link between a specific protein and a specific mental illness. Dr. Smith is engaged in which type of professional psychology?
   A. Experimental psychology
   B. Applied psychology
   C. Teaching psychology
   D. Parapsychology
   E. Pseudopsychology

4. Dr. Lee is a medical doctor who works in a hospital setting and specializes in diagnosing and treating people with psychological disorders. He can prescribe medication to help in the treatment of mental disorders. Dr. Lee is most likely a(n) _____.
   A. biological psychologist.
   B. psychiatrist
   C. mental health counselor
   D. experimental psychologist
   E. developmental psychologist

5. Dr. Jones, a developmental psychologist, has read a recent research article about children's taste preferences, which concluded that most children do not like to eat very spicy foods. When the nearby nursery school asked her advice about what to prepare for the children's snacks, Dr. Jones suggested not including any spicy foods. Dr. Jones is practicing _____ psychology?
   A. teaching
   B. experimental
   C. applied
   D. descriptive
   E. child

6. The contemporary view of psychology has evolved from all fields of study with the exception of the field of _____.
   A. economics
   B. chemistry
   C. physics
   D. philosophy
   E. biology

7. Most psychologists consider the era of modern psychology to have begun with which of the following events?
   A. Sigmund Freud begins practicing self-analysis in 1897.
   B. Wilhelm Wundt establishes a research lab to study the structures of the mind in 1879.
   C. William James textbook, Principles of Psychology, is published in 1889.
   D. John Watson and Rosalie Rayner conduct the "Little Albert Experiment" in 1920.
   E. Max Wertheimer's paper on the "Experimental Studies of the Perception of Movement" appears in 1912.

8. Functionalism is the historical school of psychology that focused its attention on _____.
   A. unconscious processes and their effect on behavior
   B. cognitive associations and how those impact learned actions
   C. the effect of the relationships between parents and children on behavior
   D. the belief that mental processes could best be understood in terms of their adaptive purpose and function
   E. the individual structures that make up the mind and how each affects and determines behavior

9. Wundt's technique of reporting one's conscious mental experiences is known as _____.
   A. introspection
   B. structuralism
   C. functionalism
   D. psychodynamism
   E. humanism

10. The behaviorist movement believed that psychology should focus on _____.
    A. dreams
    B. the totality of mental processes
    C. observable actions and associations
    D. reflexes
    E. genetics and biology

11. An introspective look at the Necker Cube illustrates that humans do not sense the world as it really is because_____.
    A. humans add personal interpretations to experiences
    B. the unconscious mind guides all of our perceptions
    C. only learned associations have meaning to an individual
    D. our free will biases our perceptions of the world
    E. behavior and mental processes are not related to perceptual processes

12. Dr. Ortiz studies the effect of neurotransmitters, chemicals that are secreted in the brain, on human behavior. She is best described as a(n) _____ psychologist.
    A. biological
    B. cognitive
    C. developmental
    D. evolutionary
    E. sociocultural

13. Dr. Amarosa is studying the relationship between the color of words presented to person and the quantity of words the person remembers. He is best described as a(n) _____ psychologist.
    A. biological
    B. cognitive
    C. developmental
    D. evolutionary
    E. sociocultural

14. Dr. Schulman believes that human behavior is generated in our unconscious minds and is the result of unresolved conflicts and desires. She views human behavior and mental processes from the _____ perspective.
    A. biological
    B. cognitive
    C. psychodynamic
    D. humanistic
    E. behaviorist

15. Which of the following statements best describes modern psychology?
    A. Psychology is a diverse field that examines issues from several perspectives.
    B. Psychology is not a valid scientific field of study.
    C. Anyone with only a bachelor's degree can be a psychologist.
    D. Psychology only explores observable actions
    E. Psychology only concentrates on mental processes

Sample Free Response Question

Respond to the following question using proper psychological terminology. Remember to define the selected terms and support your answer by referencing it to the situation posed.

Psychology is the scientific study of behavior and mental processes. The field of psychology is diverse and looks at both behavior and mental processes in different ways. Explain how each term below applies to the study of behavior and/ or mental processes. For each pair of terms, discuss the differences.

a) empirical research   b) pseudopsychology
c) psychiatrist   d) psychologist
e) experimental psychology   f) applied psychology

Sample Question Answers

Multiple Choice Answers

1. E is the correct answer. Psychology is defined as "the scientific study of behavior and mental processes."

2. B is the correct answer. The empirical approach is the standard for all psychological research because it is based on careful observation and scientifically based research.

3. A is the correct answer. Experimental psychology involves research on psychological processes.

4. B is the correct answer. A psychiatrist is a medical doctor who specializes in the diagnosis and treatment of mental disorders.

5. C is the correct answer. Applied psychology uses the knowledge developed by experimental psychologists to solve human problems. Applied psychologists "work in the field."

6. A is the correct answer. The contemporary view of psychology has evolved from the earliest philosophers and scientists, particularly biology, chemistry, and physics.

7. B is the correct answer. Wilhem Wundt established the first psychology research laboratory in Leipzig, Germany in 1879.

8. D is the correct answer. William James believed that mental processes were best understood purpose and functions.

9. A is the correct answer. Introspection was a technique used by Wilhelm Wundt in which research participants were trained in provided detailed reports of conscious mental experiences.

10. C is the correct answer. Behaviorists believed that psychology should be a completely objective science that focused only on observable behavior.

11. A is the correct answer. Personal bias and experience is involved in mental processes and behaviors.

12. A is the correct answer. The biological perspective searches for the causes of behavior in genetics, brain, nervous system, and endocrine system.

13. B is the correct answer. The cognitive perspective explains that our actions are influenced by the way we process information coming from our environment.

14. C is the correct answer. The psychodynamic perspective explains that we motivated by the energy of desires that are generated in our unconscious minds. These desires are a result of unresolved conflict, memories, and needs.

15. A is the correct answer. Modern psychology is diverse and changing very rapidly. There are nine main perspectives that underlie modern psychology. A doctoral degree is required to call yourself a psychologist.

Free Response Answer
This question would be scored using a rubric. This question has the following points:

Terms – 6 pts
Comparison – 3 pts

1. The science of psychology uses **empirical research** as the standard for all research. This means that psychological studies are scientific and based on objective and verifiable methodology and study.

2. **Pseudopsychology** is unscientific psychology that presents itself as scientific psychology.

3. Empirical research would involve studies that can be proven, such as the effects on brain damage on behavior. Pseudopsychology involves phenomenon that cannot be proven, such as fortunetelling.

4. A **psychiatrist** has a medical degree and specializes in treating people with psychological illnesses.

5. A **psychologist** has a doctoral degree and may practice in a variety of areas such as research, teaching, or therapy.

6. Psychiatrists can prescribe medication and tend not to use talk therapy as much as psychologists.

7. **Experimental psychology,** also called research psychology, conducts pure research to find new ideas in the field of psychology.

8. **Applied psychology** uses the knowledge developed in experimental psychology to solve human problems.

9. These differ in the types of research conducted as well as the arena in which they work. Experimental psychologists tend to work in labs while applied psychologists are generally found in the field. They research more practical questions.

Chapter Two – Research Methods

How Do Psychologists Develop New Knowledge?

Core Concept - <u>Psychologists like other researchers in all other sciences use the scientific method to test their ideas empirically.</u>

Psychologists use the same research tools as chemists, physicists, biologists, and doctors. The methods of study are the same; the content of that study differs. Scientists such as chemists and doctors, along with psychologists, use experiments to study their problems. In an experiment, the researcher has control over the elements involved in the experiment. All of the sciences use **empirical investigation** to answer questions. Empirical means we make a decision based on experience as opposed to making a decision based on common sense, faith, or hope. So the next time that someone says that psychology is just common sense, bring out the scientific method.

The **scientific method** allows a researcher to systematically identify a problem, design and conduct a study, examine the data, and report the results. Using the scientific method, psychologists can examine their theories. A **theory** is a testable explanation of observations. The first step in the scientific method is to develop an **hypothesis** which is a statement that predicts the outcome of a scientific study. For example, a researcher wants to see if Study Method A causes Test Score B. The researcher hypothesizes that exposure to A will cause B. The second step is to conduct a controlled test which psychologists and other scientists call an experiment. A controlled experiment is one in which the researcher directly oversees all elements of the experiment. . Because of this control, the researcher can decide cause and effect, depending on whether or not the results are statistically significant.

The researcher next gathers data. The researcher identifies the variables of importance. The **independent variable** (IV) is the variable that the researcher will manipulate (i.e. the variable that affects the behavior in question). In this study, the IV is Study Method A. The **dependent variable** (DV) is the outcome that is measured or observed. In this study, the DV is Test Score B. The researcher must also carefully define what is meant by each variable so that other researchers can replicate or repeat the study. These definitions are known as **operational definitions**. You may not agree with how a researcher defines a particular variable. The key, however, is that the researcher has determined ahead of time how each variable will be defined.

Manipulation of the IV is not always possible since psychologists often study variables such as gender or age. We cannot manipulate these types of IVs. There are other IVs that we cannot manipulate due to ethical concerns. When we cannot manipulate an IV, we are conducting a quasi-experiment. In these quasi-experimental (remember that a true experiment requires the researcher to manipulate the IV) studies we are looking at the effect of the IV on the DV. We cannot ascribe cause and effect to the IV, however. For example, does a person's gender affect that person's SAT score? Gender is the IV and SAT score is the DV. We may find an effect but we cannot find cause and effect.

After collecting all data, the scientist analyzes the results statistically and either accepts or rejects the hypothesis based on those statistical results. Results must be statistically significant if we are to accept that the IV caused the results. If results are not statistically significant, the results could have happened by chance. Even if the results are significant, there may be other explanations for the findings.

Finally, the results must be shared, often by publication or presentation. Other professionals may critique the work, or they may **replicate** (repeat) it in order to verify the results.

Sometimes the IV is not the only thing that could affect the DV. Confounding variables are extraneous variables in a study that might affect the outcome of the study. Since researchers are not always able to have complete control over everything in a participant's world, it is always possible that something other than the IV is responsible for changes that occur in the DV. For example, in our gender and SAT example, let's suppose that males get higher SAT scores. Is gender the only thing that "causes" or even contributes to higher SAT scores? It probably is not. Males tend to take more higher-level math classes, and this may be part of why they get higher SAT scores. Since we didn't study math classes as an IV, it is a confounding variable. In other words, it may be a plausible explanation for what we find.

To conduct an experiment, the researcher must identify the **population** of interest. A population for a study does not mean everyone in the world; it means the group of people in whom the researcher is interested. In our experiment on Study Methods and Grades, we will identify our population of interest as teenagers in New York City. Since we cannot study our entire population (i.e. every teen in NYC), we **sample** the population and study a small group that represents the population. Our sample should look like the teenage population. In this case we need to have male, females, as well as representative ethnicities and races.

Our sample should be randomly selected so that we eliminate the potential of volunteer bias in selection. A **random sample** means that every member of a population has an equal chance of being selected to be in the sample. One way to do this is through the use of a random number table. It is often impossible to obtain a true random sample in psychological research but it is the ideal procedure.

We then divide the sample into two groups. We use random assignment to the groups in order to avoid further bias. **Random assignment** means that everyone in the sample has an equal chance of being in each group. Each member of the sample would have a chance of being in Group A and Group B. Random assignment guards against the influence of participant characteristics.

One group is called our **control group**; the other is our **experimental group**. The experimental group will receive the treatment. In this case, they will be exposed to Study Method A. The control group does not receive any treatment. They study as usual. After a specified time period, we will see how many in the experimental group achieved Test Score B versus how many in the control group made that grade. Using statistical calculations, we will determine **statistical significance**. We look for significance levels of at least .05 and preferably .01. If we find those levels, we can conclude that Study Method A causes Test Score B.

Because this was an experiment done in a laboratory in which we controlled the environment and other potentially confounding variables, we can say with pretty good certainty that X causes Y.

Without these controls, it is difficult to determine cause and effect. All we could say is that there is a relationship between the two variables.

In some experiments, there is the potential of causing harm to the participants which is a violation of the American Psychological Association's **Code of Ethics** for Research with Human Subjects. To avoid ethical violations, researchers submit their work to **Institutional Review Boards** which review research for potential ethical issues. A similar board oversees research with animals. A major consideration for all researchers is conforming to this code and conducting ethical research. Ethical research means that we get informed consent from participants in all research, we limit deceit in research, we debrief all participants, and we do not harm them.

You can also see that it can be difficult to conduct an experiment on many topics of interest to psychologists because we cannot control the environment and there are many possible explanations for our results. Because of this limits, much of psychological research is **correlational**. Such research does not determine cause and effect but shows us the relationship between two variables. We still identify IVs and DVs, control and experimental groups but they are not manipulated and controlled as they would be in a true experiment. Often correlational research relies on intact or pre-existing groups. For these reasons we often refer to such research as a study rather than an experiment. We apply as much scientific rigor as we can within our ethical and practical limits.

There are other research designs that psychologists use to study behavior. In **survey research**, the researcher questions large groups of people about behavior and demographic characteristics and then draws correlations between variables of interest.

In **naturalistic observation**, we go to where the participants are. For instance, if we want to study the behavior of teachers, we observe them in their classrooms. We can gather descriptive information but we cannot determine cause and effect. We may conduct a **longitudinal study** over time or we may conduct **cross-sectional** or **cross-sequential** studies which eliminate the issues related to following a group of participants over time.

Core Concept - How do we make sense of the data?

How do we make sense of the data we collect? We use various statistical methods. The information we collect from participants is in the form of raw data. We have not done anything with the data. Generally we calculate **descriptive statistics** on all data. These describe the main characteristics of the data and focus on the central point about which the scores cluster. There are several measures of central tendency including the mean, the mode and the median.

Next we calculate a correlation for our data. Correlations tell us about the relationship between variables. The **correlation coefficient** does not tell us about cause and effect. It gives us information about the direction and strength of the relationship. To examine cause and effect, we use **inferential statistics**. We look for statistical significance. These numbers tell us if there is a "significant" difference between the groups that is not due to chance.

Sample Multiple Choice

1. Dr. Jordan believes there is a relationship between the amount of chocolate a child eats and the hyperactivity level of the child. This belief is a(n) _____.
   A. theory
   B. variable
   C. hypothesis
   D. paradigm
   E. premise

2. In an experiment, the variable that is manipulated is called the _____ variable.
   A. control
   B. independent
   C. dependent
   D. extraneous
   E. confounding

3. Dexter works for a magazine and is told by his editor to write an article on test scores in the local elementary school. He divides the students into groups based on grade level. He then examines the local test scores. In this study, the independent variable is the _____.
   A. school the students attend
   B. grade level of the students
   C. income level of the parents
   D. gender of the students
   E. test scores of the students

4. Dexter works for a magazine and is told by his editor to write an article on test scores in the local elementary school. He divides the students into groups based on grade level. He then examines the local test scores. In this study, the dependent variable is the _____.
   A. school the students attend
   B. grade level of the students
   C. income level of the parents
   D. gender of the students
   E. test scores of the students

5. Professor Ripken is interested in studying children's social behaviors. To do this, he visits a preschool and carefully monitors and records the children's behavior. Professor Ripken is engaged in what type of research?
   A. Survey research
   B. Naturalistic observation
   C. Case study
   D. Experimental research
   E. Longitudinal study

6. What type of research design would be used to study whether happy people are healthier?
   A. Correlational
   B. Experimental
   C. Behavioral
   D. Sociocultural
   E. Longitudinal

7. The type of bias that leads observers to expect certain outcomes is called _____ bias.
   A. confirmation
   B. expectancy
   C. personal
   D. hindsight
   E. selection

8. The _____ approves research done by psychologists at most universities.
   A. watchdog committee
   B. ethics review committee
   C. research committee
   D. institutional review board
   E. research review board

9. Rupert wants to learn whether men or women are better drivers. To determine this, he decides that he will measure driving ability by examining the number of tickets that people have been received. Thus, he is using the number of tickets as the basis of the

   _____.
   A. control group
   B. theory of good driving
   C. independent variable
   D. operational definition
   E. experimental group

10. Jason is studying visualization in high school athletes. He recruits participants from football, baseball and gymnastics at a local high school. He also recruits participants from teenagers at the mall who report sport participation. His population of interest is _____.
    A. teen at the mall
    B. all teens in the town
    C. teen athletes
    D. baseball players
    E. football players

11. Deception is allowed by the APA Code of Ethics if _____.
    A. the problem being studied is really important
    B. the participants are thoroughly debriefed
    C. the researcher is confident about his or her study
    D. no substantial risk is likely to happen to participants
    E. this study is replicating a previously completed study

12. Which of the following is a question that science cannot answer?
    A. Why do bad things happen to good people?
    B. Why do fruits go rotten in the refrigerator?
    C. Which teaching method is most effective?
    D. Which music is more popular: rap or country?
    E. Which diet is most effective in weight loss?

13. Cory scored high on a test of mathematics. He also scored high on a test of engineering. If we run a correlation on his scores, the correlation would be _____.
    A. perfect
    B. positive
    C. negative
    D. skewed
    E. nonexistent

14. Yan found a statistically significant difference in his research results. Yan used _____ statistics to find this difference.
    A. correlation
    B. descriptive
    C. inferential
    D. distributed
    E. deviation

15. Luis conducted a study of the attitudes and savings behavior. He followed 100 participants for 10 years. Luis conducted a _____ study.
    A. longitudinal
    B. ex-post facto
    C. experimental
    D. cross-sectional
    E. cross-sequential

Sample Free Response Question

Respond to the following question using proper psychological terminology. Remember to define the selected terms and support your answer by referencing it to the situation posed.

Design an experiment to determine whether a new medication will help Alzheimer's disease (AD) patients. Be sure to name and describe all of the components of an experimental study including

        a) independent, dependent, and confounding variables
        b) random sample and assignment issues
        c) control

Discuss at least two ethical issues related to the study.

Sample Question Answers

Multiple Choice Answers

1. A is the correct answer. A theory is a testable explanation of facts. Dr. Jordan's idea about chocolate and hyperactivity is testable.

2. B is the correct answer. Independent variables are manipulated by the research. It is changed on purpose by the researcher.

3. B is the correct answer. This is a quasi-experiment. While grade level is not manipulated, it is used as the independent variable that will influence the outcome variable.

4. E is the correct answer. This is a quasi-experiment. The dependent variable is the test scores of the students. It is the outcome measure and is predicted by the independent variable.

5. B is the correct answer. In naturalistic observation, the researcher goes to where the participants are. They are observed where they work or play, in their natural environment.

6. A is the correct answer. This question can only be studied by a correlational design. It is not possible to manipulate whether or not people are happy.

7. B is the correct answer. With expectancy bias, the researcher allows his or his expectations to influence or affect the outcome of the experiment.

8. D is the correct answer. Institutional Review Board is the name of the committee that screens research for potential ethical conflicts and issues.

9. D is the correct answer. An operational definition is a very clear and very precise explanation of the item being measured. It allows researchers to replicate the study and study the same variables. It removes any ambiguity in what the researcher is studying.

10. C is the correct answer. The population of interest is the group that the researcher is specifically interested in examining. In this case, the group is teen athletes. The researcher is not examining all teens, just a subset.

11. D is the correct answer. Even if participants are debriefed, the IRB must still be sure that there is no substantial risk of harm to participants. Ethics standards are more stringent these days and no harm to participants can be possible.

12. A is the correct answer. This question is one that religious leaders or philosophers try to answer. It is not one that can yield objective data.

13. B is the correct answer. If the score on one variable goes up and the score on the other variable is also high, then the correlation is positive.

14. C is the correct answer. We can only find statistical significance if we use inferential statistics which can determine if group differences are due to chance.

15. A is the correct answer. In a longitudinal study, we follow participants over a long period of time. Such studies can be expensive and time-consuming.

Free Response Answer
Free response questions are scored using a rubric. This question has the following points:

Terms: 6 points
Ethics: 2 points

Sample
1. The participants need to be identified as AD patients. There could be a control group of adults with early AD and an experimental group with moderate AD.
2. There should be some mention of some sort of sampling. It could be random sampling from a group of AD patients or random assignment to the treatment condition.

Variables
3. The independent variable must be identified as the drug (levels: drug or not).
4. The dependent variable should be identified as improvement in memory or some other improvement.
5. Confounding or extraneous variables would include level of disease, other diseases, other medications, age. Many confounds are possible.

Control
6. Sample or assignment as control should be mentioned. A placebo could also be mentioned.

Ethical Issues
7. Informed consent is problematic since the patients have dementia and may not be able to give informed consent.
8. The potential of harm of a new drug must also be considered.

Chapter Three – Biopsychology and the Foundations of Neuroscience

How Are Genes and Behavior Linked?

Core Concept – Evolution has fundamentally shaped psychological processes because it favors genetic variations that produce adaptive behaviors.

Innate (inborn) human behaviors are a result of **evolution.** Evolution is the gradual process of biological change that occurs in a species as it adapts to its environment. **Natural selection** is the driving force behind evolution, by which the environment "selects" the fittest organisms. The nature-nurture controversy explores the role of biological basis of psychology and the role of learning in psychology.

Your traits, both physical and psychological, are a combination of your genetics (heredity) and experience (environment). Taken together, heredity and environment make you unique. An organism's genetic makeup is its **genotype.** An organism's observable physical characteristics are its **phenotype.**

DNA (deoxyribonucleic acid) is a long, complex molecule that encodes genetic characteristics. **Genes** are segments of a chromosome that encode the directions for the physical and mental characteristics of an organism. Genes are the functional units of a chromosome. **Chromosomes,** which are mostly DNA, are tightly coiled structures along which the genes are organized.

Every cell in your body has 23 pairs of chromosomes that specify your hereditary makeup. Your **sex chromosomes** are the X and Y-chromosomes that determine physical sex characteristics. XY indicates a male and XX indicates a female. A gene is a portion of the chromosome that contains of DNA, which provides the chemical basis for the genetic code. This provides instructions for making a protein. Each protein influences some physical or mental characteristic.

Genetics is an exciting area with much new knowledge coming from the Human Genome Project which has mapped all of the human genes. It is important to never attribute psychological characteristics to genetics alone. Most behaviors and characteristics and even most diseases cannot be attributed to a single gene or even to specific combinations of genes. Gene mapping is not without controversy. Cloning and stem cell research have been the subject of many ethical discussions.

This area has two specialty areas. **Biopsychology** is a psychology specialty that studies the interaction of biology, behavior, and mental processes. **Neuroscience** is an interdisciplinary field that focuses on the brain and its role in psychological processes.

How Does the Body Communicate Internally?

Core Concept – The brain coordinates the body's two communications systems: the nervous system and the endocrine system. The two systems use similar chemical processes to communicate with targets throughout the body.

The **neuron** is the building block of the nervous system. A neuron is a cell specialized to receive and transmit information to other cells in the body. A neuron is also called a *nerve cell*. Bundles of many neurons are called *nerves*.

There are three types of neurons: **sensory neurons** (*afferent neurons*), **motor neurons** (*efferent neurons*), and **interneurons.** Sensory neurons are nerve cells that carry messages from sense receptors toward the central nervous system (brain and spinal cord). Motor neurons are nerve cells that carry messages away from the central nervous system toward the muscles and glands. Interneurons are nerve cells that relay messages between nerve cells, especially in the brain and spinal cord.

Glial cells are cells that bind the neurons together. They provide an insulated covering called the *myelin sheath.* It covers the axon for some neurons and facilitates the electrical impulse. A typical neuron receives thousands of messages through its **dendrites.** The dendrites are branched fibers that extend outward from the main cell body and carry information into the neuron and into the **soma** or cell body that contains the cell nucleus and the chromosomes.

When the soma becomes excited, its message is sent to the **axon**, an extended fiber that conducts information from the soma to the terminal buttons. The soma then transmits the message through an **action potential** or the nerve impulse caused by a change in the electrical charge across the cell membrane of the axon. It goes to the neuron's **terminal buttons** which are tiny bubble-like structures at the end of the axon, which contain neurotransmitters that carry the neural message into the synapse.

Nerve cells rely on electrical and chemical signals to process and transmit information. The **resting potential** occurs when the electrical charge of an axon is in its inactive state. This is when the neuron is ready to "fire." During an **action potential** the neuron "fires" and this electrical charge travels down the axon and causes neurotransmitters to be released by the terminal buttons. Neuroscientists refer to the **all–or–nothing principle** when an action potential in the axon occurs either completely or not at all. There is no almost. **Synaptic transmission** occurs when electrical messages change into chemical messages. Information crosses the **synapse** (the gap between nerve cells) when electrical impulses cause **synaptic vesicles** to burst. Chemical messengers used in neural communication called **neurotransmitters** are released.

There are many neurotransmitters. Some important neurotransmitters that are important to psychological functioning are dopamine, serotonin, norepinephrine, acetylcholine, GABA, glutamate, and endorphins. An imbalance in one or more of these neurotransmitters underlies certain disorders.

Plasticity is the nervous system's ability to adapt or change because of experience. The brain is especially good at this adaptation. When someone relearns basic processes after a head injury, the rehabilitation involve brain plasticity.

The **nervous system** is the entire network of neurons in the body. The major divisions of the nervous system are the **peripheral nervous system**, the **central nervous system**, and their subdivisions. The central nervous system is the brain and the spinal cord. The brain is responsible for decision-making, coordination, and initiating behavior. The spinal cord connects the brain to the peripheral nervous system and is responsible for **reflexes**. Reflexes are simple unlearned responses triggered by stimuli. An example of a reflex would be a knee jerk reaction to the doctor tapping your knee.

The peripheral nervous system is all parts of the nervous system lying outside of the central nervous system. It connects the central nervous system with the rest of the body through nerves. The peripheral nervous system includes the **autonomic nervous system**, which communicates with internal organs and glands, and the **somatic nervous system**, which communicates with sense organs and voluntary muscles. The autonomic nervous system has a **sympathetic division** that is arousing and helps us deal with stressful or emergency situations, and a **parasympathetic division** that is calming and returns the body to its balanced state after arousal by the sympathetic division.

The **somatic division** of the peripheral nervous system (PNS) is the brain's communication link with the outside world. It is made up of the sensory (afferent) nervous system that is responsible for sensory input and the motor (efferent) nervous system that is responsible for motor output.

The **endocrine system** is the body's chemical messenger system. **Hormones** are its chemical messengers. Hormones act like neurotransmitters in the nervous system and affect body functions as well as behavior and emotions. The endocrine system works in parallel with the parasympathetic nervous system. However in times of stress, it supports the actions of the sympathetic nervous system.

The **pituitary** or master gland tries to keep endocrine responses under control. It is attached to the brain's hypothalamus, from which it takes its orders. The pituitary gland produces hormone responses which influence the secretions of all other endocrine glands. Other glands in the endocrine system include the thyroid, parathyroid, adrenals, pancreas, ovaries, and testes.

Psychoactive drugs affect the natural chemical processes in our neural circuits by acting as **agonists,** that enhance or mimic the effect of neurotransmitters; or **antagonists** that inhibit the effects of neurotransmitters along **neural pathways.** The neural pathways are bundles of nerve cells that connect parts of the brain.

How Does the Brian Produce Behavior and Mental Processes?

Core Concept – The brain is composed of many specialized modules that work together to create mind and behavior.

In order to understand how the brain functions, scientists have developed several methods of studying the brain. An electroencephalograph or **(EEG)** is a device for recording brain waves, typically by electrodes placed on the scalp. The record produced is also called an EEG or electroencephalograph.

Brain scans are images that allow one to view the structure and function of the brain. These computerized scans have revealed that each region of the brain is specialized for its own

26

function. There are several types of scans and each type of scan has advantages and disadvantages to studying the brain. **CT scanning, or computer tomography,** creates an image of the brain using X-rays passed through the brain at various angles. **PET scanning,** or **positron emission tomography,** produces an image that shows brain activity by sensing the concentration of radioactive glucose (sugar) consumed by active brain cells. **MRI,** or **magnetic resonance imaging,** makes detailed pictures of tissues based on cell's responses in a high intensity magnetic field. An **fMRI,** or **functional magnetic resonance imaging,** is a type of MRI that reveals which parts of the brain are most active during various mental activities. Currently no single method gives biopsychologists a total picture so all types give us valuable information about the structure and functions of the brain.

The brain has three layers: the brain stem, the limbic system, and the cerebral cortex. The **brain stem** is the most primitive of the brain's three layers. It is made up of the **medulla, pons, reticular formation, thalamus, and cerebellum.** Sensory and motor pathways cross in the medulla, which means that each side of the brain connects to the opposite side of the body. The medulla also controls breathing, heart rate, blood pressure and other involuntary body functions. The pons regulates brain activity during sleep and dreaming. The reticular formation arouses the cortex to keep the brain alert and attentive to new stimulation. The thalamus is the "relay station" of the brain, where most of the brain's sensory and motor traffic is directed. The thalamus also plays a role in focusing attention. The cerebellum is responsible for coordinated movements.

The middle layer of the brain is the **limbic system.** The limbic system is involved in emotion, memory, and motivation. The limbic system includes the **hippocampus, amygdala,** and **hypothalamus.** The hippocampus is involved with long-term memory and learning. The amygdala is involved with memory and emotion, particularly fear and aggression. The hypothalamus contains important control circuits for basic motives and drives, such as hunger and eating. The hypothalamus constantly monitors blood to determine the condition of the body.

The brain's thin outer layer of gray matter is the **cerebral cortex,** which is divided into two cerebral hemispheres. The cerebral cortex is responsible for our "higher" mental processes, including thinking and perceiving.

Each of the two hemispheres of the cerebral cortex has four lobes: the **frontal lobes,** the **parietal lobes,** the **occipital lobes,** and the **temporal lobes.** The **frontal lobes** are involved with thought, speech, and voluntary movement controlled by the **motor cortex.** The **parietal lobes** are involved in the sensation of touch through the **somatosensory cortex.** These lobes also function in perceiving spatial relationships and body positions. The **temporal lobes** process sound, including speech. The temporal lobes are also involved in storing long-term memories. The **occipital lobes** house the visual cortex and are involved with vision. The **association cortex** refers to cortical regions throughout the brain that combine information from various other parts of the brain.

Cerebral Dominance refers the control over different functions that each hemisphere of the brain exerts. While this control is not absolute, many functions are "headquartered" in one hemisphere. The left cerebral hemisphere is responsible for the regulation of positive emotions, control of muscles used in speech, control of sequence of movements, spontaneous speaking and writing, remembering words and numbers, and understanding speech and writing. The right cerebral hemisphere is responsible for the regulation of negative emotions, responses to simple commands, memory for shapes and music, interpretation of spatial relationships and visual images, and recognition of faces.

The two hemispheres do communicate and cooperate with each other. The **corpus callosum** is a band of nerve cells that connect the two cerebral hemispheres. When the corpus callosum is severed, the brain is "split." This medical procedure prevents communication between the cerebral hemispheres. Split brain patients can function normally in most situations. **Roger Sperry** won the Nobel Prize in 1981 for his discoveries concerning the functional specialization of the cerebral hemispheres.

Brain damage in the right hemisphere may result in paralysis on the left side of the body, spatial and perceptual defects, impulsive behaviors, and memory deficits with performance. Brain damage in the left hemisphere may result in paralysis on the right side of the body, speech and language deficits, slow and cautious behaviors, and memory deficits with language.

There is still much to learn about the field of biopsychology with respect to how the brain works and the role of genetics in psychological processes.

Sample Multiple Choice

1. Which evolutionary principle states that a biologically based characteristic, which contributes to the survival of a species, will increase in a population over time because those who lack the characteristic are likely to pass on their genes than those who have the gene?
   A. Neuroscience
   B. genotype
   C. Natural selection
   D. Heritability
   E. Phenotype

2. Mary has blue eyes and blonde hair. What aspect of Mary's genetics does this describe?
   A. Genotype
   B. Phenotype
   C. Sex chromosome
   D. Genetic mutation
   E. Natural selection

3. Taylor's sex chromosomes are XY. Which of the following is a true statement about Taylor?
   A. Taylor is female.
   B. Taylor is male.
   C. Taylor's sex cannot be determined from this information.
   D. Taylor probably inherited a genetic mutation.
   E. Taylor's future behavior will be unusually aggressive.

4. Which of the following statements is true regarding genetics and an individual's psychological characteristics?
   A. Genetics has contributed little to the understanding of human behavior and mental processes.
   B. Genetics only influences behavior, not mental processes.
   C. Genetics only influences mental processes, not behavior.
   D. Psychological characteristics are attributed to genetics alone.
   E. Psychological characteristics are not attributed to genetics alone.

5. Specialized cells that make up the basic building blocks of the nervous system are called
   _____.
   A. axons
   B. synaptic vesicles
   C. neurons
   D. glial cells
   E. dendrites

6. The nerve cells that carry messages away from the central nervous system to the muscles are called _____.
   A. interneurons
   B. glial cells
   C. sensory neurons
   D. motor neurons
   E. afferent neurons

7. When a neuron fires and its electric charge travels down the axon, causing neurotransmitters to be released by the neuron's terminal buttons, a(n) _____ happens.
   A. action threshold
   B. action potential
   C. reuptake
   D. resting potential
   E. synaptic transmission

8. Serotonin and dopamine are examples of chemical messengers used in neural communication. These chemical messengers are known as _____.
   A. potassium inhibitors
   B. hormones
   C. neurotransmitters
   D. efferent neurons
   E. soma

9. Morphine is a chemical that mimics the action of endorphins. Morphine is a(n) _____.
   A. endorphin agonist
   B. endorphin antagonist
   C. dopamine agonist
   D. serotonin antagonist
   E. serotonin agonist

10. The ability of one structure of the brain to adopt the functions of a part that has been damaged best illustrates the concept of _____.
    A. all-or- nothing principle
    B. synaptic transmission
    C. brain plasticity
    D. reflexes
    E. hemispheric specialization

11. The part of the central nervous system that is responsible for thinking, judgment, planning, and decision making is the _____.
    A. sympathetic division
    B. parasympathetic division
    C. brain
    D. pituitary gland
    E. somatic division

12. The division of the autonomic nervous system that calms the body down after arousal and returns the body to a balanced internal condition is the _____.
    A. sympathetic division
    B. parasympathetic division
    C. somatic division
    D. spinal cord
    E. brain

13. Mary's doctors performed a brain scan that used a radioactive solution of glucose to trace her brain's activity. Mary had a(n) _____.
    A. fMRI
    B. MRI
    C. PET scan
    D. CT scan
    E. EEG

14. Steven's heartbeat and breathing cannot be regulated. His doctors are convinced that there is damage to his nervous system. What area of the brain are Steven's doctors likely to find responsible for this?
    A. Thalamus
    B. Hypothalamus
    C. Amygdala
    D. Hippocampus
    E. Medulla

15. Ashley is a 20-year-old woman who cannot remember her street address and is having trouble learning new things. Her neurologist will focus on her _____.
    A. thalamus
    B. hypothalamus
    C. amygdala
    D. medulla
    E. hippocampus

Sample Free Response Question

Respond to the following question using proper psychological terminology. Remember to define the selected terms. Support your answer by referencing the situation posed.

Sam is a hockey player who gets a concussion. Explain how a biopsychologist or a neuroscientist would explain his injury using these terms. Be sure to also define each term.
    a) glial cells
    b) fMRI
    c) cerebral dominance
    d) autonomic nervous system
    e) synaptic transmission

Sample Question Answers

<u>Multiple Choice Answers</u>

1. C is the correct answer. Natural selection is the driving force behind evolution, by which the environment "selects" the fittest organisms.

2. B is the correct answer. An organism's phenotype is the organism's observable physical characteristics.

3. B is the correct answer. The XY sex chromosome pair indicates a male.

4. E is the correct answer. An individual's psychological characteristics are determined by many factors including environment, not genetics alone.

5. C is the correct answer. Neurons, or nerve cells, are the building blocks of the nervous system.

6. D is the correct answer. Motor neurons, or efferent neurons, carry messages way from the central nervous system to the muscles and glands.

7. B is the correct answer. An action potential is a nerve impulse caused by a change in the electrical charge across the cell membrane of the axon, causing the release of neurotransmitters.

8. C is the correct answer. Neurotransmitters relay neural messages across the synapse. Neurotransmitters include serotonin, GABA, dopamine, among many others.

9. A is the correct answer. Agonists enhance or mimic the effect of neurotransmitters.

10. C is the correct choice. Brain plasticity helps the nervous system adapt to physical damage.

11. C is the correct answer. The brain is the central nervous system organ responsible for the central executive life functions such as thinking, planning, and decision making.

12. B is the correct answer. The parasympathetic division is the part of the autonomic nervous system that returns the body to calmer functioning after arousal.

13. C is the correct answer. A PET scan traces the brain's activity by tracing a radioactive form of glucose.

14. E is the correct answer. The medulla is the brain-stem structure that controls breathing and heart rate.

15. E is the correct answer. The hippocampus is the limbic system structure involved in long term memories.

<u>Free Response Answer</u>
This question would be scored using a ten-point rubric. This question has the following points:

Terms – 5 pts
Application – 5 pts

1. Glial cells are neuronal support cells that bind neurons together.
2. Glial cells insulate the covering of the neuron (myelin sheath) and aid in the speed of neural transmission. They would aid in Sam's movement.
3. An fMRI is a type of scan that uses magnetic waves to determine functioning.
4. An fMRI shows what parts of the brain are most active during various mental activities. Doctors would use this to determine what injury has occurred to Sam.
5. Cerebral dominance refers to each brain hemisphere having control over different functions of the body.
6. It would be important to know what is happening in Sam's hemispheres. Lateralization is important for his handedness.
7. Autonomic nervous system is the part of the peripheral nervous system that communicates between the central nervous system, internal organs and glands.
8. The autonomic nervous system is divided into the sympathetic and parasympathetic divisions, which arouse and calm the body, maintaining homeostasis. Both are important for his playing as he starts and stops play.
9. Synaptic transmission is the relaying of information across the synapse.
10. During synaptic transmission, electrical messages are changed into chemical messages that are carried by neurotransmitters. For instance, dopamine and norepinephrine are responsible for alertness and energy.

Chapter Four – Sensation and Perception

How Does Stimulation Become Sensation?

Core Concept – <u>The brain senses the world indirectly because the sense organs convert stimulation into the language of the nervous system: neural messages.</u>

It is difficult to separate sensation and perception. Think of sensation as the physical experiences of stimuli, and think of perception as the psychological interpretation of those stimuli. Can you see why it would be difficult to separate these two?

How is this transformation accomplished since the brain does not receive stimulation? It is through the process of transduction that physical energy such as light waves is transformed into neural messages. The process begins when the body detects some physical stimulus such as a light wave caused when you turn on a lamp. When this stimulus reaches the sensory organ (e.g. the eyes) receptors or specialized neurons are activated. Their excitation is converted to a nerve signal.

The process is similar to what happens when you go to the grocery store and used the scanner. A light flashes as you move the canned peas across the scanner. The lines on the code on the peas are changed into an electronic signal that is read by the scanner attached to the computer. For us, the nerve signal travels along a sensory pathway to the thalamus to specialized processing areas.

We face a huge amount of incoming stimuli all day long. It would overwhelm us and our processing system if our sensory systems were not able to adapt. Think about walking into a darkened movie theater. At first, you cannot see much of anything. Yet, if you wait a few minutes, your eyes adjust and you can easily find your friends and see the seats. Sensory adaptation allows this. It is the diminishing response to protracted stimulation. The stimulation has receded into the background without your noticing it unless the stimulus changes in some way. Note, however, that if a stimulus is painful or exceedingly intense, adaptation may not occur.

There are other important principles you should know when discussing sensation. One is the absolute threshold. This is the small amount of stimulus that an organism can detect. Your absolute threshold is not absolute, though. The distinction between detecting a stimulus and not detecting it can be vague. Another principle is the difference threshold. This is the smallest difference between two stimuli that you can recognize. For example, you are in a room with every light on. Your brother thinks the room is too bright. If your brother turns off a small side lamp, you will probably not notice the difference. How many lamps would have to be turned off before you did notice a difference? When you recognize a small difference, it is called the just noticeable difference (JND). The terms JND and difference threshold are used interchangeably.

It is important to note that the JND is different for each sense. Psychologists who studied the JND in different senses found that the size of the difference is related to the intensity of the stimulus. This is called Weber's law. Weber's law means that if you have on every light in a room, you would have to turn off several of them if you are to notice a difference. Two other "laws" relate to stimulus detection. Fechner's law says that increases in the physical magnitude of a stimulus produce smaller increases in perceived magnitude. Steven's power law also deals with magnitude estimation. It is more accurate than Fechner's law.

The study of thresholds is a part of signal detection theory. This theory helps us understand why the thresholds are not constant and how individual characteristics affect detection.

How Are the Senses Alike? How Are They Different?

Core Concept – <u>The senses all operate in much the same way but each extracts different information and sends it to its own specialized processing region in the brain.</u>

The senses are very similar in many ways but quite different in many others. Each sense is designed differently but each sends neural messages to specific parts of the brain. Vision is the sense that we understand the best. We often use the analogy of a camera when we talk about the eye. The eye takes in light through the pupil, focuses it in the lens and converts or transduces the signal in the retina. Much of the work of the retina occurs in the photoreceptors. One type of receptor, the rods, is most sensitive to light. The other type, cones, processes color. Sensation occurs in the eyes; perception occurs in the brain. In the visual cortex, neural impulses are transformed into color, form and movement.

There are two major theories of how we see color. The trichromatic theory says we have 3 receptors for color: red, green and blue. The opponent-process theory explains color by processing that occurs in the bipolar cells. This theory explains some color blindness as well as afterimages, sensations that linger after the stimulus is removed.

Hearing is another sense about which we know a good amount. Hearing begins with sound waves that are produced by vibrations. Frequency and amplitude are the two characteristics of a sound wave. Frequency is the number of cycles completed by a wave in a given time. Amplitude refers to the height of the wave, a measure of its physical strength. Sound waves first enter the outer ear and hit the tympanic membrane (eardrum). Next the waves are transmitted to three bones called the hammer, anvil, and stirrup. The vibrations pass to the cochlea and the basilar membrane in the inner ear. The cochlea is the primary hearing organ. The basilar membrane converts the waves into neural messages which then travel to the auditory cortex. Pitch (high or low quality), loudness, and timbre (mix of tones) are three psychological components of sound.

Our other major sense are the vestibular (balance and gravity) sense, the kinesthetic (body position and movement) sense, smell, taste, and skin senses or touch. Pain is sometimes listed as an additional sense. The gate-control theory explains pain control as a function of a neural "gate" that blocks incoming pain signals. Studying how people deal with pain often focuses on the use of placebos or fake drugs. Often people have the same response to a placebo as to a "real" medication.

Subliminal persuasion is the idea that very weak stimulation that you don't notice can affect your beliefs and behavior. It relates to the concept of thresholds. No controlled research study has ever demonstrated that subliminal messages can influence behavior.

What is the Relationship between Sensation and Perception?

Core Concept – <u>Perception brings meaning to sensation, so perception produces an interpretation of the world, not a perfect representation of it</u>.

Perception is our interpretation of the sensations. Our percepts are what we perceive, the meaning we attach to the sensations. There are several ways in which we attach meaning to sensations. We have specialized groups of cells in the brain whose purpose is to detect certain features of stimuli. These feature detectors are still somewhat of a mystery to most psychologists.

We know that we process stimuli in different ways as well. In bottom-up processing, or stimulus-driven processing, the characteristics of a stimulus are attended to first. Our percept is determined by these features. In top-down processing, we incorporate our past knowledge, expectations, goals, culture and motivation to interpret a stimulus. The perceptual constancies help with perception. This is the ability to recognize objects as the same or constant under different environmental condition. We see our desk as the same regardless of the light in the room.

One way to examine sensation and perception is to look at illusions which occur when our mind tricks us and perceives a stimulus in an incorrect way. Psychologists use ambiguous figures, images that can have more than one correct interpretation, to study perception. Gestalt theory also helps us understand perception. Gestalt psychology began in German and the word "gestalt" loosely translated means form, shape, or put together. The Gestalt laws of perception help to explain why we see things as we do.

Figure/ground says that the figure, usually in the foreground, will stand out and capture our attention. In ambiguous figures, these elements can reverse, giving us a totally different perception. With closure, we fill in the blanks of any missing information so that we see a whole. The laws of perceptual grouping, similarity, proximity, continuity, and common fate help us cope with large amounts of stimuli. Many Gestaltists believe these laws are built into the brain although the exact mechanisms of perception are still being debated.

The Gestalt laws of grouping help us to group items together to form a percept, the meaningful product of perception. The general law of Pragnanz says we see the simplest pattern possible. We focus on the meaningfulness of the whole, rather than the individual components. The law of similarity says that we group like items together. This law is used by grocery stores in their end displays. All we see is the soda or cookies. We do not see individual packages. Another law is the law of proximity which says that we group items that are close to one another. The law of common fate involves items that are in motion. We group together items that are moving in the same direction. Think about the geese flying south for the winter. We see the triangle or whatever shape they make, rather than individual birds.

Another aspect of perception that is important is depth perception. The development of depth perception is an interplay of genetic programming and learned behavior. Depth perception first appears around the age of six months. Some depth cues depend on the use of both eyes. Among these binocular cues are convergence and retinal disparity. Some depth perception cues involve only one eye. Among these monocular cues are relative size, interposition, and relative motion.

Some of perception involves learning-based inferences. We use prior experience and learning when we interpret sensory information. We use this prior learning to make an inference or assumption about what the sensation means. Generally such inferences are pretty accurate. However, those ambiguous figures mentioned earlier as well as illusions can lead to incorrect conclusions. In addition to our expectations formed by experience, context is an important element in forming perceptions. When we see fireworks, we assume that it is a holiday, probably July 4th. Perceptual set is also involved in our percepts. We are primed to expect certain cues and interpret them in certain ways. On the highway, if you see a series of brake lights ahead, you assume it is either an accident or a speed trap.

Culture also influences perception. Where you live when you grow up influences your perceptions about straight lines and height. A person who has grown up where there are few large buildings, airports, or tunnels will experience the Ponzo illusion differently from someone who has grown up in a big city.

Thus we actually have two competing theories of perception: learning theory and innate theory. Our perception is influences by both nature and nurture. We know that the brain is predisposed to certain perceptions but that others are clearly learned. Thus, perception is an interaction of nature and nurture.

Sample Multiple Choice

1. The _____ receptors convert incoming stimulus information into electrochemical signals.
   A. brain
   B. perceptory
   C. sensory
   D. neural
   E. stimulus

2. The part of the eye most directly involved in transduction is the _____.
   A. retina
   B. cerebellum
   C. fovea
   D. cornea
   E. iris

3. You are sitting in the Student Union listening to your radio but you forgot your earphones. The person at the next table asks you to turn down the volume. The smallest amount that you can turn down the volume but still hear it is known as the _____ threshold.
   A. difference
   B. absolute
   C. perceptual
   D. phonological
   E. audible

4. Some stores have reported that the subliminal messages played in stores to prevent shoplifting are successful. However, research does not support this finding. The most likely explanation for the success reported is _____,
   A. there was no good merchandise in the store
   B. the stores did not have accurate records
   C. the research was not really accurate
   D. the shoplifters just did not get caught
   E. employees in those stores were more vigilant

5. The _____ cells are responsible for collecting impulses from photoreceptors and shuttling them to the ganglion cells.
   A. bipolar
   B. retinal
   C. rod
   D. foveal
   E. cone

6. Anna developed an ear infection. The most likely place in the ear for this infection is in the _____.
   A. cochlea
   B. anvil
   C. stirrup
   D. auditory nerve
   E. auditory cortex

7. Susan developed an inner ear infection and her doctor told her to refrain from driving until it is cured. The sense, aside from hearing, most affected by this infection would be the _____ sense(s).
   A. olfactory
   B. kinesthetic
   C. vestibular
   D. skin
   E. visual

8. You are walking through the perfume department in a store where Christmas carols are playing when you have a sudden memory of your grandmother. The sense most associated with memory is _____.
    A. vision
    B. kinesthetic
    C. sound
    D. taste
    E. smell

9. You cannot stand the taste of brussel sprouts. You would most likely be classified as a(n) _____.
    A. supertaster
    B. nontaster
    C. sensitive taster
    D. extreme taster
    E. moderate taster

10. You go to a restaurant for dinner and the waiter gives you five choices of salad dressing. When you choose the one you want for your salad you are using _____ processing.
    A. choice
    B. decision
    C. top-down
    D. bottom-up
    E. cortical

11. You run into your psychology professor at a baseball game after you have completed his course. You cannot remember why you know him. This illustrates the concept of _____.
    A. context effect
    B. functional fixedness
    C. perceptual set
    D. cultural influence
    E. memory

12. When we hear the melody in a song as opposed to the individual notes in the song, we are using the Gestalt law of _____.
    A. continuity
    B. Pragnanz
    C. proximity
    D. perceptual grouping
    E. similarity

13. If you hold your finger about twelve inches from your face and look at it first with your right eye and then with your left eye, you will see it differently. This is due to the depth cue of
_____.
    A. convergence
    B. retinal disparity
    C. relative size
    D. proximity
    E. interposition

14. You read about a plane that crashed off the shore of the local beach. It was a hazy night and there were no lights. One reason for the crash could be the perceptual cue of _____.
    A. convergence
    B. atmospheric perspective
    C. retinal disparity
    D. relative size
    E. interposition

15. Sharon had trouble hearing the teacher so the school gave her a hearing test. Some of the sounds presented were at such a low level of intensity that she could hardly hear them. These sounds were below her _____.
    A. absolute threshold
    B. hearing threshold
    C. difference threshold
    D. discriminative threshold
    E. adaptive threshold

Sample Free Response Question

Respond to the following question using proper psychological terminology. Remember to define the selected items. Support your answer by referencing the situation posed.

Explain how a dancer would make use of each of the following senses in the spring recital. Describe an interaction that might occur between at least two senses.
            a) vision
            b) hearing
            c) kinesthetic
            d) vestibular
            e) skin senses

Sample Question Answers

Multiple Choice Answers

1. C is the correct answer. Stimuli are converted in the sensory receptors. The impulses are neural and the process is called transduction.

2. A is the correct answer. The retina is the light sensitive layer of cells where transduction occurs.

3. A is the correct answer. The difference threshold is the smallest amount of change in sound that can be detected half the time.

4. E is the correct answer. There is no research evidence to support subliminal persuasion. Most likely, employees were watching more carefully after the reports.

5. A is the correct answer. The bipolar cells collect impulses from the rods and cones and then "shuttle" them to the ganglion cells.

6. A is the correct answer. The cochlea is the primary sound organ. It is filled with fluid and is the most likely place for an infection.

7. C is the correct answer. The vestibular sense relates to body position and gravity. When we get an ear infection, our sense of balance can be affected.

8. E is the correct answer. The sense of olfaction, or smell, is most linked to emotional memories.

9. A is the correct answer. A supertaster has more taste buds for bitter flavors and is more sensitive to strong tasting foods such as brussel sprouts.

10. C is the correct answer. You are most likely to choose a salad dressing based on expectations of taste and other cognitive factors rather than on the characteristics of the dressing such as ingredients.

11. A is the correct answer. Context effect relates to recognizing people when they are in the situation in which you normally see them. Thus, when you encounter the professor outside of the classroom, you do not recognize him.

12. E is the correct answer. Similarity occurs when we group like items (e.g. the notes in the song) together rather than perceiving them individually.

13. B is the correct answer. Retinal disparity is a binocular depth cue. We see greater disparity with close objects.

14. B is the correct answer. Haze makes objects in the distance look fuzzy. This phenomenon is known as atmospheric perspective.

15. A is the correct answer. Your absolute threshold is the amount of stimulus necessary for you to detect it.

Free Response Answer
This question would be scored using a seven-point rubric. This question has the following points:

Senses – 5 points.
1. Vision is one of the primary senses as she looks at the other dancers and the stage as well as the audience.
2. Hearing would come into play as she listens to the music and the other dancers.
3. The kinesthetic sense, that of movement, would be primary. She feels the correct steps.
4. The vestibular sense is involved in balance.
5. The skin sense or touch would also be important as she moves around the stage and as she dances with a partner. Even the feel of the shoes or costume would be important.

Interaction – 2 pts
6 & 7. Hearing and kinesthesia often interact as do hearing and the vestibular sense. Vision can also interact with kinesthesia as movement might be impeded by what is seen.

Chapter Five – States of Consciousness

How is Consciousness Related to Other Mental Processes?

Core Concept – <u>Consciousness can take many forms, while other mental processes occur simultaneously outside our awareness.</u>

Consciousness is the process by which the brain creates a model of internal and external experience. Studying consciousness is difficult because it is subjective and very difficult to quantify. Psychological study of consciousness re-emerged in the 1960s because many psychological issues needed a better explanation than behaviorism provided. New technology allowed scientists to study models of how the brain processes information.

The connection between mental processes and the brain is the focus of cognitive neuroscience. **Cognitive neuroscience** is an interdisciplinary field involving cognitive psychology, neurology, biology, computer science, linguistics, and specialists from other fields. Conscious processes require attention. **Nonconscious processes** have no attention restrictions. Nonconscious processes are any brain processes that do not involve conscious processing. These processes include preconscious memories and unconscious processes.

Several tools are used to study consciousness. *PET scans* show how different regions of the brain become active during different conscious tasks. Shepard and Metzler's *mental rotation* experiment showed that people took longer to decide whether images were the same or different, as the angles through which each pair was rotated. Kosslyn's research examined zooming in on mental images. It showed that the smaller the detail one asked for in describing a mental image, the longer it took to elicit a response. People needed extra time to zoom in on a mental image to resolve smaller features.

Consciousness has three important functions: restriction, combination, and manipulation. It restricts our attention. Consciousness provides a place where sensation combines with memory, emotions, motives, and other psychological processes. Consciousness allows manipulating our environment, rather than just responding to the environment.

The unconscious mind has two main divisions, the preconscious and the unconscious. **Preconscious** memories are not currently in one's consciousness, but they can be recalled into consciousness voluntarily or after something calls attention to them. The **unconscious** refers to cognition occurring without awareness. Priming is an example of unconscious processing. In Freud's psychoanalytic theory, the unconscious mind makes up the major part of the mind. It serves as a source of sexual and aggressive desires.

What Cycles Occur in Everyday Consciousness?

Core Concept – <u>Consciousness changes in cycles that correspond to our biological rhythms and to the patterns of stimulation in our environment.</u>

Daydreaming is a common variation of consciousness in which attention shifts to memories, expectation, desires, or fantasies and away from the immediate situation. We also have biological cycles the influence our sleep cycle. **Circadian rhythms** are physiological patterns that repeat approximately every twenty-four hours, such as the sleep –wake cycle. The main events of sleep include REM sleep (including sleep paralysis) and non-REM sleep.

REM sleep is a sleep stage that occurs approximately every ninety minutes and is marked by bursts of sudden eye movements occurring under closed eyelids. **Sleep paralysis** normally occurs during REM sleep. This is a condition in which the sleeper is unable to move any of the body's voluntary muscles, except those controlling the eyes. REM sleep periods are associated with dreaming. **Non-REM sleep** includes the recurring periods, mainly associated with the deeper stages of sleep, when a sleeper is not showing rapid eye movement.

The **sleep cycle** progresses through several distinct phases. When we are fully awake, EEG patterns show fast brain waves called *beta waves*. When we are drowsy, EEG patterns show *alpha waves*. Stage 1 sleep, is characterized by *theta waves* and fast brain (*beta*) waves that are seen in the waking state. Sleep spindles, the sudden bursts of fast electrical activity, characterize Stage 2 sleep. During stages 3 and 4, the deepest sleep occurs and *delta waves* appear.

The deepest point in the sleep cycle occurs in Stage 4, about a half hour after the onset of sleep. As Stage 4 ends, the electrical activity in the brain increases, and the sleeper climbs back up through the sleep stages in reverse order. As the sleeper reaches stage 1 again, fast beta waves reappear. The sleeper now enters REM sleep for the first time. After a few minutes of REM sleep, the entire cycle begins to repeat itself. In a typical night, the deepest sleep, stages 3 and 4, occurs mainly in the first few hours. As the night progresses, the sleeper spends more and more time in the stages of light sleep and REM sleep.

Most adults need 8 hours of sleep. **REM rebound** is a condition of increased REM sleep caused by REM-sleep deprivation. When a sleeper is deprived of REM sleep on a given night, the next day the person is tired and irritable. The following night, the sleeper spends much more time in REM sleep than usual. As we age, REM sleep diminishes. **Sleep debt** is a sleep deficiency caused by not getting enough sleep for optimal functioning.

Scientists have long studied dreams and the function they serve. There are many explanations for dreaming. **Freud's dream theory** states that dreams serve two purposes: to guard sleep (by disguising disturbing thoughts with symbols) and serve as wish fulfillment. Freud explored dreams in terms of **manifest content** (the storyline of a dream) and **latent content** (the symbolic meaning of objects and events in a dream).

Dreams vary by culture, gender, and age. Dreams may be a source of creative insight. Sleep research shows that dream content frequently connects with recent experiences. Dreams relate to cognitive experiences, such as memory. The **activation-synthesis dream theory** states that dreams are the brain's attempt to make sense of (synthesize) random electrical activation coming from the brain stem.

There are several sleep disorders. **Insomnia** is the most common sleep disorder and involves insufficient sleep, inability to fall asleep, frequent arousals, or early awakenings. **Sleep apnea** is a respiratory disorder in which the person intermittently stops breathing several times while asleep. **Night terrors** occur mainly in children and involve deep sleep episodes that produce vivid and terrifying images that are usually forgotten upon awakening. **Narcolepsy** produces sudden daytime sleep attacks and is usually accompanied by **cataplexy** (a sudden loss of muscle control).

What Other Forms Can Consciousness Take?

Core Concept – An altered state of consciousness occurs when some aspect of normal consciousness is modified by mental, behavioral, or chemical means.

Hypnosis is an induced state of awareness, characterized by heightened suggestibility, deep relaxation, and highly focused attention. Hypnosis is explained as a dissociative state that parallels normal consciousness. Hypnosis is used in pain relief, and in some psychological treatment (posthypnotic amnesia**). Meditation** is induced by focusing on a repetitive behavior, assuming certain body positions, and minimizing external stimulation. It produces relaxation and sense of well- being.

Psychoactive drug states are achieved when psychoactive drugs enter the body. Psychoactive drugs are chemicals that affect mental processes and behavior by their effects on the brain. **Hallucinogens** (including mescaline, psilocybin, LSD, PCP, and cannabis) are drugs that create hallucinations or alter perceptions of the external environment and inner awareness. **Opiates** (including morphine, heroin, codeine, and methadone) are highly addictive drugs that produce a sense of well-being and are strong pain relievers.

Depressants are drugs (including barbiturates, benzodiazepines, rohypnol, and alcohol) that slow down mental and physical activity by inhibiting transmission of nerve impulses in the central nervous system. Physical dependence, tolerance, and addiction to alcohol often begin with binge drinking which is common on many campuses. **Stimulants** (including amphetamines, methamphetamine, MDMA/ecstasy, cocaine, nicotine, caffeine) are drugs that arouse the central nervous system, speeding up mental and physical responses.

Dependence and addiction occur because most psychoactive drugs mimic neurotransmitters or enhance or weaken their effects at synapses. The reduced effectiveness a drug has after repeated use is called **tolerance**. **Physical dependence** is a process by which the body adjusts to, and comes to need, a drug for its everyday functioning. **Psychological dependence** is a desire to obtain or use a drug even though there is no physical dependence. **Addiction** occurs when a person continues to use a drug, even though there are adverse effects on the person's health or life. **Withdrawal** refers to the uncomfortable physical and mental symptoms that occur when a drug is discontinued.

Consciousness occurs in many forms. Mental processing can also occur outside of consciousness. The precise mechanisms of consciousness are not yet fully understood.

Sample Multiple Choice

1. Consciousness includes which of the following states?
   A. Sleeping
   B. Hypnosis
   C. Daydreaming
   D. Reading
   E. All of the above

2. As you are studying your text, you are probably not thinking about what you ate for dinner last night. The memory of what you had for dinner last night is most likely located in your
   _____.
   A. nonconscious
   B. preconscious
   C. hypnogogic state
   D. collective unconscious
   E. conscious

3. Stage _____ of sleep is characterized by EEG readings that indicate the presence of sleep spindles and K-complexes.
   A. Stage 1
   B. Stage 2
   C. Stage 3
   D. Stage 4
   E. REM

4. When _____ is disrupted, jet lag occurs.
   A. stage 4 sleep
   B. REM sleep
   C. circadian rhythms
   D. stage 1 sleep
   E. K-complexes

5. Most dreaming occurs during the sleep stage of _____.
   A. stage 1
   B. stage 2
   C. stage 3
   D. stage 4
   E. REM

6. REM sleep is sometimes referred to as "paradoxical sleep" because _____.
   A. people can speak very eloquently when in REM sleep
   B. night terrors are common
   C. muscles in the body remain relaxed while the brain and the eyes remain active
   D. muscles in the body become rigid and the brain and eyes are in a very relaxed state
   E. REM sleep is unnecessary for healthy daily functioning

7. John had a dream in which he imagined that he was sitting in his psychology class wearing only his underwear. After discussing this dream with his best friend, John determined that this dream represents his anxiety about not doing well in his psychology class. This aspect of John's dream is best explained by _____.
   A. manifest content
   B. latent content
   C. activation-synthesis theory
   D. information processing theory
   E. cataplexy

8. The sleep cycle is approximately _____ long.
   A. sixty minutes
   B. thirty minutes
   C. eight hours
   D. ninety minutes
   E. twenty-four hours

9. Mary had stayed up all night cramming for her psychology test. The following day, she is tired and irritable. What will Mary likely experience when she sleeps that night?
   A. Night terrors
   B. Somnambulism
   C. Narcolepsy
   D. REM rebound
   E. Nightmares

10. Recent studies of hypnosis have indicated that hypnosis _____.
   A. can increase pain tolerance
   B. can improve memory by at least 50 percent
   C. can make people do things they would never do in their everyday lives
   D. has no value to people lives
   E. is just as effective as medication for almost all physical illnesses

11. The _____ theory of hypnosis states that hypnotic effects occur because people act out desired roles.
   A. dissociation
   B. social
   C. behavioral
   D. divided consciousness
   E. information-processing

12. Larry starts drinking one beer every time he goes on a date because he says that it relaxes him. Eventually, Larry needs more beer to achieve the same level of relaxation. Larry is experiencing _____.
    A. withdrawal
    B. tolerance
    C. psychosis
    D. denial
    E. the placebo effect

13. Alcohol is classified as a(n) _____.
    A. depressant
    B. stimulant
    C. hallucinogen
    D. antagonist
    E. agonist

14. How do psychoactive drugs affect perceptual processes and behavior?
    A. They work via heightened suggestibility.
    B. They use the placebo effect.
    C. They alter neural activity in the brain.
    D. They work only on psychological processes.
    E. They work only on physical processes.

15. All of the following are stimulants except _____.
    A. heroin
    B. caffeine
    C. ecstasy/MDMA
    D. cocaine
    E. nicotine

Sample Free Response Question

Respond to the following question using proper psychological terminology. Remember to define the selected terms and support your answer by referencing it to the situation posed.

The experiences of sleeping, dreaming, and experiencing altered states of consciousness have fascinated people for many years. Explain what each is and how each of the following relates to contemporary research and theory about sleeping, dreaming, and altered states of consciousness.
    A. Sleep debt
    B. Activation-synthesis theory
    C. Insomnia
    D. Physical addiction
    E. Opiates

Sample Question Answers

Multiple Choice Answers

1. E is the correct response. Choices A through D are example of conscious processes.

2. B is the correct answer. Preconscious memories can be recalled into consciousness after something calls attention to it.

3. B is the correct answer. Stage 2 sleep is characterized by sudden bursts of electrical activity, called sleep spindles.

4. C is the correct answer. Circadian rhythms are physiological patterns that repeat approximately every twenty-four hours.

5. E is the correct answer. REM sleep is the stage when most dreaming occurs.

6. C is the correct answer. Muscles do not move, but the brain and eyes are active during REM sleep

7. B is the correct answer. The latent content is the symbolic representation and meaning of dreams.

8. D is the correct answer. The sleep cycle is approximately ninety minutes long.

9. D is the correct answer. REM rebound occurs when there has been a lack of REM sleep.

10. A is the correct answer. Hypnosis is helpful to some people in pain management.

11. B is the correct answer. This theory states that hypnotic effects occur because an individual acts out desired social roles.

12. B is the correct answer. Tolerance is the gradual need for an increased quantity of a substance to achieve a desired effect.

13. A is the correct answer is the correct answer. Alcohol is a substance that decreases neural activity in the central nervous system.

14. C is the correct answer. Psychoactive drugs alter the neural activity in the brain which alters perceptual processes and behaviors.

15. A is the correct answer. Heroin is classified as an opiate.

<u>Free Response Answer</u>
This question would be scored using a rubric. The question has the following points

Terms - 5 points
Applications - 5 points

1. Sleep debt is an individual's lack of necessary hours of sleep.
2. Sleep debt impairs daily functioning and can slow reaction time.
3. Activation-synthesis theory is a dream theory that states that dreams are the brain's attempt to make sense of random electrical activity coming from the brain stem.
4. It is one of several current dream theories. Studying and documenting this theory has become easier as tools for studying the brain, such as the fMRI, have become more sophisticated.

5. Insomnia involves the inability to fall asleep, stay asleep, or avoid frequent awakenings during your sleep. It is the most common sleep disorder.
6. Current research has developed drugs to help cure insomnia. Current research has also examined the impact of sleeplessness on society.

7. Physical addiction is the body's inability to function without a specific drug. Physical addiction is the result of drug tolerance and is often accompanied by psychological addiction.
8. Current research has examined the physical mechanism underlying addiction as well as examining the genetic components of addictive behavior.

9. Opiates are drugs produce a sense of well-being and are strong pain relievers. Opiates are highly addictive drugs.
10. Research has examined beneficial ways to use these drugs as well as ways to lessen their addictive quality.

Chapter Six – Learning

Learning is a concept that is defined very broadly by psychologists. It is commonly defined as a relatively permanent change in behavior based on experience. It is a change in a behavior or behavior potential that must be relatively consistent. It is a process based on experience and interaction with the environment. It does not include changes that occur due to **maturation**. For example, pubertal changes are maturational. Some learning occurs in formal contexts such as school while other learning occurs through observing others.

Learning can occur with either behavior or with mental processes. The behaviorists believe the learning only occurs with behavior since they can observe behavior. The cognitive psychologists think that is a limiting view and that learning requires them to make inferences about mental processes that we cannot see.

Contrasting with learned behavior is instinctive behavior. This type of behavior is often called species-typical behavior. Such behaviors are not greatly influenced by experience. Human behavior is much more influenced by learning that is the behavior of most other animals. Learning can be simple or complex. **Habituation** is learning not to respond to a stimulus that is repeated. Humans also tend to prefer stimuli to which they have previously been exposed, even if those stimuli were unpleasant. Marketers use this **mere exposure effect** in creating advertising.

There are two general approaches to learning theory. One is behavioral which involves either classical conditioning or operant conditioning. The second approach is cognitive learning which focuses on insight and imitation.

What Sort of Learning Does Classical Conditioning Explain?

Core Concept – Classical conditioning is a basic form of learning in which a stimulus that produces an innate reflex becomes associated with a previously neutral stimulus which then acquires the power to elicit essentially the same response.

Classical conditioning is a form of learning in which two stimuli become associated. Pavlov's work with his dog was the most famous classical conditioning experiment and the theory was based on reflexes. **Reflexes** are triggered by stimuli and have a biological basis. In that experiment, his dog came to associate the sound of the bell with dinner and thus he learned to salivate. When you read Pavlov's study, keep in mind that conditioned means learned and unconditioned means unlearned.

Pavlov found that when he paired a neutral stimulus that did not normally provoke a reflex with a natural reflex-producing stimulus, there was a learning effect. The neutral stimulus began to evoke the reflex responses. There are several elements involved in classical conditioning. An **unconditioned stimulus** (UCS) elicits a reflexive behavior which is called an **unconditioned response** (UCR). The neutral stimulus (NS) does not produce any response. When the NS is presented repeatedly at the same time as the UCS, it becomes a **conditioned stimulus** (CS). This CS then will produce a **conditioned response** (CR), which is similar to the UCR or reflex. It is often a weaker version of the CR. The process by which the UCR becomes a CR is called **acquisition**. Timing is critical as the UCS and the NS must be presented very close in time if the association is to occur.

This learned behavior can be eliminated or **extinguished** if the CS is presented repeatedly without the UCS. However, sometimes the conditioned response reappears unexpectedly. That is called **spontaneous recovery**. This occurrence is particularly relevant to therapists who study fear and anxiety. **Stimulus generalization** occurs when similar stimuli are presented and the conditioned response takes place. However, a person can learn to respond to stimuli that are similar in **stimulus discrimination**. The person learns to respond to one stimulus but not to others that are similar.

There are many applications of classical conditioning. John B. Watson and Rosalie Rayner conducted a notorious study called Little Albert in which they classically conditioned a toddler to fear a white rat. They also conditioned him to fear anything that looked like the rat including Santa Claus and his beard. They did not **countercondition** (pairing relaxation with the stimulus that is feared) him so we do not know if Little Albert retained the fear. Food aversions are another example of classical conditioning in "real-life."

Psychoneuroimmunology explores the use of classical conditioning with the immune system. Psychologists are currently studying the role of conditioning in taste aversion and chemotherapy patients.

How Do We Learn New Behaviors by Operant Conditioning?

Core Concept – In operant conditioning, the consequences of behavior such as rewards and punishments influence the chance that the behavior will occur again.

Operant conditioning was introduced at the start of the twenty-first century. While B.F. Skinner is credited as being the father of operant conditioning, his ideas were based upon work by Edward Thorndike who found that behavior is controlled by its consequences. It is learned through trial and error. He called this the **law of effect**.

B.F. Skinner extended Thorndike's theory. Skinner believed that behavior is explainable by looking outside the individual not inside, that behavior is determined by the environment. He looked at conditions that follow and strengthen responses. He studied his theory using an **operant chamber**, a boxlike apparatus that can be programmed to deliver reinforcement. This chamber is often called a "Skinner box." He even used such a box in the raising of his daughter.

The central idea of operant conditioning is that behavior becomes more or less likely depending on its consequences. A response can lead to three types of consequences: neutral consequences, reinforcement, (increases the probability that the response it follows will recur), or punishment (makes the response it follows less likely to recur). Consequences are most effective when they capitalize on inborn tendencies.

Both positive and negative reinforcers increase the likelihood of a response. With **positive reinforcement**, something pleasant is presented. With **negative reinforcement**, something unpleasant is removed. The word negative is used in the mathematical sense of subtracting. There are many ways of using these **reinforcement contingencies**.

Studies have shown that **continuous reinforcement**, rewarding every correct response, is very effective when learning a new skill. It is also useful in shaping new behaviors since increasingly complex behaviors can be rewarded. Once the desired behavior is established, intermittent or partial reinforcement will maintain the new behavior. Behavior is more resistant to extinction with **intermittent reinforcement**. As in classical conditioning, **extinction** of behavior can occur in operant conditioning.

Intermittent reinforcement occurs in two main schedules. One is ratio which is based on the number of responses. Interval schedules reward after a specified time. **Fixed ratio** schedules occur when reinforcement is given after a predetermined number of responses. In a **variable ratio** schedule, the number of responses required for reinforcement fluctuates. With a **fixed interval** schedule, reinforcement occurs after a specified time while in **variable interval** schedules, the timing of the reinforcement varies.

Reinforcers that fulfill biological needs are **primary reinforcers**. Not all reinforcers fulfill such needs. For instance, money is a strong reinforcer but in and of itself has no value. It has its value because of what it can buy. It is a **secondary** or **conditioned reinforcer** that has acquired its reinforcing power. Conditioned reinforcement is the principle behind the **token economy** used in many mental institutions.

Researchers have discovered that the chance to engage in activities that are desirable can be a strong reinforcer. A preferred activity can be used to reinforce a less preferred one. Educational institutions and parents have used this principle for a long time. Psychologists know that the **Premack Principle** is at work when a child does chores to earn praise from a parent.

Does operant conditioning apply across cultures? Researchers have shown that the basic principles do work across cultures although the reinforcers vary. Because secondary reinforcers are learned through association with other reinforcers and are acquired through learning, people from different cultures tend to view secondary reinforcers differently. Money, attention, praise, and even good grades are values in our culture as secondary reinforcers (that is, they motivate most people's behavior). These things may not have the same meaning for people from other cultures. Someone from a collectivistic culture may not value praise for an individual but rather praise for a group effort. Similarly, punishments may be viewed differently by people from different cultures. Disapproval or fines may work in one culture but not in another. Thus, the principles involved in operant conditioning remain invariant but the manifestation and content is relatively fluid and may change from one culture to another.

Punishment occurs when an aversive stimulus, or one that is disliked, is used to weaken the behavior it follows. In **positive punishment** an aversive stimulus is applied. In **negative punishment**, a reinforcer is removed. The goal in punishment is always to extinguish an undesired behavior. Punishment and negative reinforcement may sometimes look similar.

However, each has a totally opposite goal in terms of their result. Punishment is used to decrease a behavior while negative reinforcement is used to increase a behavior.

It is important to remember that punishment is not terribly effective. When the threat of punishment is removed, the behavior usually returns. Research has shown that reinforcement is more successful in changing behavior. In limited situations, though, punishment can be effective. If punishment is the only option, there are several conditions that should be met. Punishment should be immediate and consistently administered every time the unwanted behavior occurs. It should be limited in time and intensity. In other words, it should be just enough to stop the behavior. Punishment should target the specific behavior and specific situation. Negative punishment is more effective than positive punishment.

How do classical and operant conditioning compare? The first difference is in the consequences of the behavior. They also differ in the sequence of the stimulus and response. Classical conditioning relies on past experience while operant conditioning uses future reinforcement to encourage desired behavior. Operant conditioning focuses more on new behaviors while classical conditioning focuses on eliciting the same responses to new stimuli. The process of extinction also works in a slightly different manner in each. In classical conditioning we extinguish a behavior by withholding the UCS while in operant conditioning, the behavior is under the control of the responder. These processes are not opposite explanations for behavior. They can work in a complementary fashion.

How Does Cognitive Psychology Explain Learning?

Core Concept – According to cognitive psychology, some forms of learning must be explained as changes in mental processes, rather than as changes in behavior alone.

We do not see the mental processes behind learning. During World War I, Wolfgang Kohler examined the behavior of chimpanzees. He showed that the animals could solve complex problems when they combined simple behaviors that they had previously learned. He believed that the chimps solved these problems by reorganizing their perceptions of the problem, a process he named **insight learning**.

Edward Tolman expanded the study of insight learning by examining **cognitive maps** in rats. A cognitive map is a mental representation of a physical space. Tolman also demonstrated that this learning could occur without reinforcement. He called this latent learning. Tolman's work was a challenge to the behaviorists. Recent studies have pointed to the hippocampus as the brain structure involved in constructing cognitive maps.

Albert Bandura added the idea that we learn vicariously or by observing others, noticing the consequences and modifying behavior accordingly. This type of learning is called **social learning** or observational learning. A model's behavior is most influential when the behavior is seen as having reinforcing consequences, and the model is liked and respected and is seen positively. There are perceived similarities between the model and the observer and the model's behavior must be visible. Social learning is not unique to humans.

Social learning has been the focus of multiple studies on media and violence. Over fifty studies have shown a correlational relationship between violent television and aggression. More than a hundred studies have suggested a causal relationship, due to what psychologists call psychic numbing.

Recently cognitive psychologists have added a cognitive component to behavioral learning. Rescorla has shown that the most critical feature of a conditioned stimulus is its informativeness, or its value in predicting when the unconditioned stimulus will occur. Kamin expanded this concept and demonstrated that a CS-R connection will only occur if the CS contains unique information about the UCS. Other researchers have studied the role of cognition in operant conditioning. They have shown that reinforcement changes expectations as well as behavior.

There are also brain functions at work in learning. Learning involves physical changes as the synapses between nerve cells are strengthened in a process called **long-term potentiation**. Parts of the limbic system that are rich in dopamine receptors are involved in the brain's sense of reward. Some researchers are proposing two types of learning circuits in the brain that may divide the type of learning that occurs.

Sample Multiple Choice

1. The story of Sabra overcoming her fear of flying and getting the job illustrates the concept of
   _____.
   A. good luck
   B. learning
   C. hard work
   D. skill
   E. talent

2. The type of learning in which association plays a major role is _____.
   A.   classical conditioning
   B.   instinctual learning
   C.   operant conditioning
   D.   social learning
   E.   insight learning

3. When you learn to ignore the sounds of traffic on the busy street where you live, you are
   exhibiting _____.
   A. unlearning
   B. habituation
   C. conditioning
   D. instinct
   E. prompting

4. You were conditioned to smile when you hear Christmas carols. During the summer, this response diminishes. However, in November when you hear these songs, you begin to smile again. In classical conditioning, the return of this response is known as _____.
   A. acquisition
   B. extinction
   C. reconditioning
   D. spontaneous recovery
   E. generalization

5. You were frightened by a yellow cat when you were a child. Now you get scared whenever you see any cat. In classical conditioning, this response would be known as _____.
   A. spontaneous recovery
   B. discrimination
   C. generalization
   D. insight
   E. extinction

6. Dr. Susie has a client who is exhibiting an undesirable conditioned fear. Susie decides to try a therapeutic strategy called _____ conditioning to extinguish the response.
   A. appetitive
   B. aversive
   C. reflex
   D. stimulus
   E. counter

7. Your psychology professor gives several scheduled short quizzes and three scheduled tests throughout the semester. She is using a _____ schedule of reinforcement.
   A. fixed interval
   B. variable ratio
   C. fixed ratio
   D. variable interval
   E. continuous

8. Stimuli that fulfill basic needs and act as a reinforcer are called _____ reinforcers.
   A. secondary
   B. natural
   C. conditioned
   D. primary
   E. neutral

9. Punishment is designed to _____ a behavior while negative reinforcement is designed to _____ a behavior.
   A. increase, decrease
   B. extinguish, repeat
   C. highlight, emphasize
   D. repeat, extinguish
   E. decrease, increase

10. The lights in your house went out and it was pitch dark in your house. You were able to navigate to the kitchen because of a _____ map.
    A. navigation
    B. cognitive
    C. memory
    D. representation
    E. environmental

11. You are in the grocery store waiting to check out. You son cries because he wants candy. When you give in to his demands to make the tantrum stop, he has been _____.
    A. positively reinforced
    B. socially reinforced
    C. negatively reinforced
    D. positively punished
    E. classically conditioned

12. Your teacher says that if everyone stays quiet for the next thirty minutes, the class would have no homework. This is an example of _____.
    A. positive reinforcement
    B. negative reinforcement
    C. classical conditioning
    D. positive punishment
    E. negative punishment

13. Kohler's study of chimpanzees suggests that they reorganize their perceptions, a mental process he called _____ learning.
    A. operant
    B. latent
    C. classical
    D. insight
    E. perceptual

14. Jack learned how to shoot a free-throw by watching his older brother. Bandura called this _____ learning.
   A. insight
   B. latent
   C. imitational
   D. perceptual
   E. observational

15. The part of the brain most implicated in the development of cognitive maps is the _____.
   A. thalamus
   B. hippocampus
   C. hypothalamus
   D. limbic system
   E. cerebellum

Sample Free Response Question

Respond to the following question using proper psychological terminology. Remember to define the selected terms and support your answer by referencing the situation posed.

There have been many studies of television violence and aggressive behavior. Explain how there could be a relationship between the two variables by defining and explaining the applicability of each of the following terms:
   a) positive reinforcement
   b) negative reinforcement
   c) punishment
   d) observational learning

Sample Question Answers

Multiple Choice Answers

1. B is the correct answer. Learning is a lasting change in behavior that results from experience.

2. A is the correct answer. In classical conditioning, a previously neutral stimulus becomes associated with an unconditioned response. The neutral stimulus becomes a conditioned stimulus, evoking a conditioned response.

3. B is the correct answer. Habituation is learning not to respond to a stimulus that is repeatedly presented.

4. D is the correct answer. In spontaneous recovery, a response that has been extinguished reappears after a time delay.

5. C is the correct answer. In generalization, a conditioned response to one stimulus is extended to similar stimuli.

6. E is the correct answer. Counterconditioning is a therapeutic technique that teaches clients to relax in response to a fear or anxiety-provoking stimulus.

7. A is the correct answer. Because the quizzes and tests are scheduled, the professor is using a fixed interval schedule. You are reinforced after a predetermined time.

8. D is the correct answer. Primary reinforcers have an innate basis, such as biological value, to their reinforcing power.

9. E is the correct answer. Punishment is designed to decrease a behavior while negative reinforcement is designed to increase a behavior.

10. B is the correct answer. A cognitive map is a mental representation of a physical space.

11. A is the correct answer. Because your son got what he wanted when he cried, his crying has been reinforced and is likely to reoccur. Because he was given something (candy), the reinforcement is positive.

12. B is the correct answer. The teacher is trying to get the behavior of being quiet to repeat. She is taking away an aversive stimulus (homework) if the behavior is repeated. This is an example of negative reinforcement.

13. D is the correct answer. Insight learning is a form of cognitive learning whereby perceptions are suddenly reorganized.

14. E is the correct answer. Observational learning is a form of cognitive learning in which new responses are acquired by watching someone else's behavior.

15. B is the correct answer. Brain imaging studies have pointed to the hippocampus as instrumental in "drawing" cognitive maps.

Free Response Answer
This question would be scored using a rubric. This question has the following points:

Definitions – 4 pts
Explanation/Application – 4 pts

1. Positive reinforcement is presenting a stimulus after a behavior to encourage that behavior to repeat.
2. When someone acts aggressively after viewing violence on television, they may be positively reinforced by encouragement from others.

3. Negative reinforcement is the removal of an unpleasant stimulus if a desired behavior repeats.
4. Often, someone who behaves aggressively after viewing violent television gets attention. The unpleasantness of being ignored is removed, thus encouraging the aggressive behavior.

5. Punishment is the imposition of a stimulus to extinguish a behavior.
6. Because punishment is not terribly effective, it does not stop the aggression that follows viewing violence for long.

7. Observational learning is a form of cognitive learning in which new responses are acquired after watching others.
8. This form of learning explains aggressive behavior that follows watching violent television, especially if the actors receive attention or fame. In addition, if the actor is popular, imitation is even more understandable.

Chapter Seven – Cognition

What is Memory?

Core Concept – Human memory is an information-processing system that works constructively to encode, store, and retrieve information.

The **information-processing model** is a cognitive understanding of memory, emphasizing how information is changed when it is encoded, stored, and retrieved. **Encoding** involves changing information so that the information fits into the preferred memory system. Encoding requires selection, identification, labeling, and sometimes elaboration. **Storage** involves the retention of encoded material. Memory storage occurs in stages. **Retrieval** involves the location and recovery of information from memory. **Eidetic memory**, or photographic memory, is a rare type of extremely clear and persistent form of memory.

How Do We Form Memories?

Core Concept – Each of the three memory stages encodes and stores memories in a different way, but they work together to transform sensory experience into a lasting record that has a pattern or meaning.

The *Atkinson and Shiffrin model of memory* explains that memory is divided into three stages. **Sensory memory** is the first of the three memory stages that saves brief sensory impressions of stimuli. Characteristics of sensory memory include a storage capacity of about 12–16 items, a duration of about ¼ second, a structure that involves a separate sensory register for each sense, and a biological basis of separate sensory pathways that feed into working memory. There is a separate sensory register for each sense. Iconic memory stores images while echoic memory stores sounds.

Working memory (including short-term memory or STM) is the second of the three memory stages, and the most limited in its storage capacity. It preserves events for less than one minute without rehearsal. Working memory is involved in control of attention, attaching meaning to stimulation, and making associations among ideas and events. The storage capacity of STM is 5–9 items ("Magic 7+/- 2"). It can hold information for about twenty seconds. Because of the limits of time and capacity, it is important to have tools to work with information in this stage.

Chunking (organizing large pieces of information into smaller, more meaningful units) and **maintenance rehearsal** (repetition and review of material in STM) function in working memory. **Elaborative rehearsal** occurs when information is actively reviewed and related to information already in long-term memory. They use the central executive processes to direct attention to information from the other two parts. The phonological loop involves acoustic **encoding** whereby working memory changes information into sound patterns. Finally, the sketchpad is used to store visual images visual and spatial encoding.

The **levels of processing theory** and experiments (Craik and Lockhart, Craik and Tulving) explained that words that were processed more deeply for meaning were remembered better than words examined for rhymes or for target letters.

Although the exact biological mechanisms of working memory are not clear, scientists have discovered that the biological basis of working memory is the hippocampus and the frontal lobes. Brain imaging studies have differentiated the executive processes of working memory as anatomically distinct from the sites of short-term storage.

Working memory encodes information and then transfers that information to long-term memory. **Long-term memory (LTM)** is the third of the three memory stages, with the largest capacity and the longest duration. LTM stores information according to meaning. It has an unlimited storage capacity and duration.

Long-term memory is divided into **procedural memory** (how things are done) and **declarative memory** (fact memory). Declarative memory is divided into **semantic memory** (language, facts, general knowledge, concepts) and **episodic memory** (personal events and experiences).

Karl Lashley studied the **engram or memory trace**. The engram is the physical change in the brain that is associated with a memory. The amygdala are crucial to forming new memories. **Consolidation** is the process by which short-term memories change to long-term memories. Amnesia is the inability to form memories. **Anterograde amnesia** is the inability to form new memories and **retrograde amnesia** is the inability to remember old memories. A **flashbulb memory** is a clear and vivid long-term memory of an especially meaningful and emotional event.

How Do We Retrieve Memories?

Core Concept – Whether memories are implicit or explicit, successful retrieval depends on how they were encoded and how they are cued.

Implicit memories are memories that are not deliberately learned or those of which you have no conscious awareness. **Explicit memories** have been processed with attention and can be consciously recalled. There are several ways in which memories can be retrieved.

Retrieval cues are stimuli that are used to bring a memory into consciousness or into behavior. **Priming** is a technique for cueing implicit memories by stimulating a memory without awareness of the connection between the cue and the retrieved memory. Explicit memories are retrieved through two main processes. The first is **recall,** when someone must reproduce previously presented information. The second is **recognition,** when someone must identify present stimuli as having been previously presented.

Other factors that affect retrieval include the **encoding specificity principle** and **mood-congruent memory**. The encoding specificity principle states that context affects the way a memory is encoded and stored, influences its retrieval. The more closely the retrieval cues match the form in which the information was encoded, the better the information will be remembered. Mood-congruent memory is a memory process that selectively retrieves memories that match one's mood. The **TOT (tip of the tongue) phenomenon** is fairly common and frustrating. The TOT phenomenon is the inability to recall a word, while knowing that the word is in memory.

Why Does Memory Sometimes Fail Us?

Core Concept – Most of our memory problems arise from memory's "seven sins" – which are really by-products of otherwise adaptive features of human memory.

Daniel Schachter looked at reasons why our memory sometimes fails us. He suggests there are seven reasons or "sins" that cause us to forget. **Transience** is based on the idea that long- term memories gradually weaken over time. **Ebbinghaus' Forgetting Curve** is a graph illustrating that the greatest amount of forgetting occurs during the first day after learning and then reaches a plateau, below which little more is forgotten. **Absent-mindedness** is forgetting caused by lapses in attention.

Blocking is caused by *interference* and is forgetting that occurs when an item in memory cannot be accessed or retrieved. There are two types of inference. In **proactive interference,** earlier learning interferes with memory for later information. In **retroactive interference,** new information interferes with memory for information learned earlier. The **serial position effect** is a form of interference related to the sequence in which information is presented. Generally, items in the middle of the sequence are remembered less well than items presented first (primacy effect) or last (recency effect).

Misattribution is a memory fault that occurs when memories are retrieved, but are associated with the wrong time, place, or person. They are put in the wrong context. **Suggestibility** occurs when external cues distort or create memories. It is the process of memory distortion as the result of deliberate or inadvertent suggestion.

The **misinformation effect** is the distortion of memory by suggestion or misinformation as was found in the Loftus and Palmer studies. *False memories* are created through credible suggestions. These studies have relevance for eyewitness testimony. Factors that affect the accuracy of eyewitness testimony include the use of leading questions, time, reconstructed memory, and the age of the witness. The validity of recovered memories is controversial. The idea of buried memories related to trauma was first raised by Freud. Cognitive research suggests otherwise. Emotionally charged memories tend to be remembered. However, the issue of recovered memories remains controversial.

The sixth "sin" is bias. **Bias** refers to the influence of attitudes, personal beliefs, and experiences on memory. **Expectancy bias** is the tendency to distort recalled events to make them fit one's expectations. The self-consistency bias states that we are more consistent in our attitudes, opinions, and beliefs than we actually are. **Persistence** is a memory problem in which unwanted memories cannot be put out of our minds.

Mnemonics are techniques for improving memory by making connections between new material and information already stored in long-term memory. The method of loci is a mnemonic technique that involves associating items on a list with a sequence of familiar physical locations. **Natural language mediators** are words associated with new information to be remembered. Memory is flexible, personal, and creative. Memory ultimately works by meaningful associations.

How Do Children Acquire Language?

Core Concept – <u>Infants and children face an especially important developmental task with the acquisition of language.</u>

Language is the ability to communicate through spoken and written words and gestures. The *innateness theory of language* explains that children acquire language not merely by imitation but by following an inborn program of steps to acquire the vocabulary and grammar of the language of their environment. Chomsky explains this through the **language acquisition device or LAD.** The LAD is a biologically organized mental structure in the brain that facilitates the learning of language because it is innately programmed with some of the fundamentals of grammar. The LAD contains some basic rules, common to all human languages. The Human Genome Project has provided some evidence for the genetic basis of the foundations of language.

The babbling stage is a foundation for language acquisition in which babies make nearly all of the sounds heard in all languages. Children develop vocabulary and **grammar,** the rules of language that specify how to use words, morphemes, and syntax, to produce understandable sentences, in three initial stages. The three stages of acquisition are the *one word stage, two word stage, and telegraphic speech.* **Morphemes** are meaningful units of language that make up words. Phonemes are sounds that make up words. **Overgeneralization** is applying a grammatical rule too widely which results in creating an incorrect form of the word.

When children are about eighteen months old, word learning accelerates rapidly. Children begin to "name" items. After about six months, children begin to use language to convey more complex ideas. Cross-cultural studies have identified three categories of idea that are common to children: movers, locations and moveable objects. Children also have to learn the social rules of conversation. Both these rules and language are most easily learned in early childhood.

What Are the Components of Thought?

Core Concept – <u>Thinking is a cognitive process in which the brain uses information from the senses, emotions, and memory to create and manipulate mental representations, such as concepts, images, schemas, and scripts.</u>

The idea that the brain is an information-processing organ that operates like a computer is called the **computer metaphor**. Psychologists use this metaphor to explain both memory as well as cognition.

Concepts are mental representations of categories of items or ideas, based on experience. **Natural concepts** are the mental representations of objects or events from our personal experience. A **prototype** is the ideal, or best example, of a concept category. **Artificial concepts** are defined by rules as with a mathematics formula.

Concept hierarchies organize levels of concepts from most general to most specific. Cultural differences exist in thought processes. The biggest differences have been seen in logic and in concept formation. Some cultures put less emphasis on precise definitions and allow more fluid boundaries.

Imagery adds complexity and richness to thinking. *Cognitive mapping* is mental imagery of a physical location. You should remember Tolman's work on cognitive maps. Cognitive and other mental maps reflect our subjective impressions. Thus, there can be cultural influences that develop from our own perspectives.

The biological processes involved in thought are studied through event-related potentials. **Event-related potentials** are brain waves shown in an EEG in response to stimulation.

Schemas are knowledge clusters or general conceptual frameworks that provide expectations about topics, events, objects, people, and situations. Schemas are used in our expectations and for making inferences. **Scripts** are clusters of knowledge about sequences of events and actions expected to occur in particular settings. Scripts may have conflicting information or a cultural bias.

What Abilities Do Good Thinkers Possess?

Core Concept – Good thinkers not only have a repertoire of effective strategies, called algorithms and heuristics, they also know how to avoid the common impediments to problem solving and decision-making.

Effective problem solving involves identifying the problem and selecting a strategy. **Algorithms** are problem-solving strategies that guarantee a correct outcome, if correctly applied. **Heuristics** are cognitive shortcuts used to solve complex mental tasks. They do not guarantee a correct solution. Useful heuristic strategies include working backwards, searching for analogies, and breaking a big problem into smaller problems.

Some obstacles to problem solving include **mental set** (the tendency to respond to a new problem in the same way as you responded to an old problem), **functional fixedness** (the inability to perceive a new use for an object associated with a different purpose), self-imposed limitations, lack of knowledge, lack of interest, low self-esteem, fatigue, drug use, and stress.

Judgment and decision-making are influenced by many factors. Poor judgment and decision making are commonly caused by many types of bias. **Confirmation bias** is paying attention to outcomes that support our beliefs and ignoring evidence that contradicts our beliefs. **Hindsight**

bias is the tendency, after learning about an event, to believe that you could have predicted the event in advance. **Anchoring bias** is a faulty heuristic caused by basing an estimate on an unrelated quantity. The **representative bias** is a faulty heuristic strategy in which once something is categorized, it shares all of the features of other members in that category. The **availability bias** is another faulty heuristic strategy that estimates probabilities based on information that can be recalled from experience.

Creativity is a mental process that produces novel responses that contribute to the solution of problems. The most creative individuals have the most expertise in their fields. **Aptitudes** or innate potentialities for creativity include independence, intense interest in a problem, willingness to restructure a problem, preference for complexity, a need for stimulating interaction.

Sample Multiple Choice

1. The three stages of the Atkinson-Shiffrin information processing memory model are
   _____.
   A. hippocampus, thalamus, amygdala
   B. input, process, output
   C. sensory memory, working memory, long term memory
   D. shallow processing, parallel processing, deep processing
   E. semantic memory, declarative memory, procedural memory

2. An example of episodic memory is _____.
   A. telling someone how to ride a bike
   B. answering correctly in your history class that Delaware was the first state to ratify the U.S. Constitution
   C. knowing that the word for hello in Spanish is *hola*
   D. remembering that you got a puppy for your seventh birthday
   E. remembering how to complete a math problem using long division

3. John was running late for a date, when his mother asked him to pick up some things from the store for her. John did not want to be bothered writing out a list to help him remember the items. John's mom asked him to bring home milk, cheese, butter, eggs, paper towels, apples, and cereal. Which of the following is John most likely to forget to bring home?
   A. milk
   B. cereal
   C. paper towels
   D. eggs
   E. John will remember everything because there are fewer than 9 items

4. Which of the following is a true statement according to the levels of processing theory?
   A. The most forgetting occurs forty-eight to seventy-two hours after learning the information and then markedly increases.
   B. Rehearsal encodes memories from sensory memory to long term memory automatically.
   C. Deep processing involves elaborate rehearsal, which transfers memories from working memory into long term memory.
   D. There are two levels of processing: procedural and iconic.
   E. We can only process between five and nine items into our long term memory.

5. The brain structure responsible for transferring memories from short-term memory into long-term memory is the _____.
   A. hypothalamus
   B. thalamus
   C. hippocampus
   D. frontal lobes
   E. cerebellum

6. Noam Chomsky believes which of the following regarding how children acquire language?
   A. He believes they acquire it by imitation only.
   B. It happens more rapidly if the household is bilingual.
   C. They have an innate ability to acquire language.
   D. Positive reinforcement allows for language development.
   E. They must learn to speak through interaction with social role models.

7. Which of the following statements is an example of grammatical overgeneralization?
   A. I goed to my house yesterday.
   B. Dog cute.
   C. The car is sad.
   D. We like 'ookie.
   E. Bye-bye.

8. Which of the following statements would be true if someone was listening to the babbling of children from the United States, Japan, Brazil, and Uruguay?
   A. No difference in the babbling could be heard.
   B. Children from the United States would babble at a faster rate than the others.
   C. Children from Japan would babble at a faster rate than the others.
   D. The listener could tell the children apart if they were older than six months of age.
   E. The listener could tell the children apart at any age.

9. You download a great new recipe for chocolate cheesecake. The recipe looks complicated, but the site guarantees that if you follow the directions exactly, you have a great dessert. Following the exact ingredients and steps is an example of _____.
   A. an algorithm
   B. an heuristic
   C. the availability bias
   D. functional fixedness
   E. an event script

10. It is sometimes preferable to solve a problem using heuristics rather than an algorithm because _____.
   A. algorithms are shortcuts that can save time
   B. heuristics guarantee correct solutions to problems
   C. heuristics save time with problem solving
   D. heuristics prevent fixation
   E. algorithms are usually not dependable

11. How many morphemes does the word "untied "have?
   A. one
   B. six
   C. three
   D. two
   E. four

12. A rose has all of the features that are associated with a flower. A rose can be considered a(n) _____.
   A. prototype
   B. social script
   C. phoneme
   D. morpheme
   E. heuristic

13. An example of functional fixedness is _____.
   A. failing to use a quarter as a screwdriver when you are putting together your dorm fan
   B. not being able to solve your math problem because you are applying the same rule and you keep getting the wrong answer
   C. using your sweatshirt as a pillow
   D. substituting applesauce for oil in a cake recipe
   E. making pancakes for dinner, instead of chicken

14. You were told that Taylor is an engineer and Alex is a kindergarten teacher. When you meet your new neighbors for the first time, you assume that Alex is the wife and Taylor is the husband, rather than the actual situation—Alex is the husband and Taylor is the wife. What does this situation illustrate?
   A. Availability bias
   B. Confirmation bias
   C. Representativeness bias
   D. Anchoring bias
   E. Problems with working memory

15. After a plane crashes, airlines notice a drop in reservation rates because people overestimate the frequency of these disasters. What does this illustrate?
   A. Availability bias
   B. Confirmation bias
   C. Representativeness bias
   D. Anchoring bias
   E. Social schemas

Sample Free Response Question

Respond to the following question using proper psychological terminology. Remember to define the selected terms and support your answer by referencing it to the situation posed.

Marcy has just moved into her new college dorm. She is making adjustments moving to a new place and meeting new friends. Define each of the following terms and explain how each could apply to Marcy's new situation.

> a) Chunking
> b) Episodic memory
> c) Retroactive interference
> d) Prototype
> e) Representativeness bias

Sample Question Answers

Multiple Choice Answers

1. C is the correct answer. The three stages of the Atkinson-Shiffron model are sensory memory, working (STM) memory, and long–term memory (LTM).

2. D is the correct answer. Episodic memory is long term memory for personal events.

3. D is the correct answer. According to the serial position effect we are most likely to forget non-novel items in the middle of a list.

4. C is the correct answer. Information is transferred from STM to LTM through rehearsal.

5. C is the correct answer. The hippocampus is the brain structure most associated with transferring memory from STM into LTM.

6. C is the correct answer. The innateness theory of language describes the LAD as the language acquisition mechanism for children as they develop.

7. A is the correct answer. Overgeneralization is applying a grammatical rule too widely which results in creating an incorrect from of the word.

8. A is the correct answer. The babbling stage is the foundation for language when young babies make almost all of the sounds heard in every language.

9. A is the correct answer. A recipe is an example of an algorithm as it is a foolproof step by step plan to get the correct desired outcome when followed properly.

10. C is the correct answer. Heuristics are mental shortcuts.

11. C is the correct answer. "Un" has meaning, "tie" has meaning, and "d" has meaning. Morphemes are meaningful units of the word "untied."

12. A is the correct answer. A rose is a best example of the concept of flower.

13. A is the correct answer. Functional fixedness is not being able to think about an object in a way that is different from how the object was intended to be used.

14. C is the correct answer. Your experience with kindergarten teachers is most likely with someone who is female.

15. A is the correct answer. The availability bias is misinformation based on facts that can be the most easily recalled.

Free Response Answer
This question would be scored using a rubric. The question has the following points:

Terms- 5 points
Applications-5 point each

1. Chunking is taking large pieces of information and breaking down that information into smaller units for storage in STM.
2. An example of this could be Marcy's student ID number – if it is 1123456, Marcy could remember 112-34-56.

3. Episodic memory is a type of LTM (declarative) that involves personal events and experiences.
4. Marcy may see a fellow student in the dorm who looks like her cousin.

5. Retroactive interference occurs when new information interferes with previously learned material.
6. This may happen to Marcy when she is trying to remember her new dorm address and can only remember her home address.

7. A prototype is a best example of a concept.
8. Marcy may be enrolled in Introduction to Psychology, a prototype of an introductory collegiate course.

9. Representativeness bias is a faulty heuristic strategy in which once something is categorized, it then shares all of the features of other members in that category
10. Marcy may see an older person wearing a suit and glasses and assume it is her professor, rather than a classmate.

Chapter Eight – Emotion and Motivation

What is an emotion? An emotion is a four-part process involving physiological arousal, subjective feelings, cognitive interpretation, and behavioral expression. All of these elements interact. How is motivation linked to emotion? They are complementary processes. Emotion emphasizes arousal while motivation emphasizes how this arousal becomes action.

What Do Our Emotions Do For Us?

Core Concept – <u>Emotions have evolved to help us respond to important situations and to convey our intentions to others.</u>

From an evolutionary perspective, emotions are adaptive. They help us cope with important situations. They have survival value and have been shaped by natural selection. Individuals vary greatly in emotional responsiveness. Some of these differences come from random genetic variations and some are learned. Thus we have learned emotional responses combined with a biological predisposition for others.

There is some universality to certain emotional expressions. Paul Ekman found that people around the world understand essentially the same facial expressions. There are major differences, though, in the context and intensity of emotional display across cultures. These are the display rules.

How many emotions are there? Robert Plutchik posits an "emotion wheel" with eight primary emotions in the inner wheel. Variations of those eight emotions form the outer circle. Paul Ekman has identified seven basic emotions. Certain emotions, however, are not universal and they can carry different meanings in various cultures. Some researchers have examined gender differences in emotion. However, it is difficult to separate the biological roots of these differences from the learned cultural components.

Where Do Our Emotions Come From?

Core Concept – <u>The discovery of two distinct brain pathways for emotional arousal has clarified the connection among the many biological structures involved in emotion and has offered solutions to many of the long-standing issues in the psychology of emotions.</u>

There are two distinct emotion processing systems in the brain. One is the fast response system which operates mainly at the unconscious level or away from our awareness. This system screens incoming stimuli and helps us to respond quickly. This system is linked to implicit memory.

The other emotional system functions at the conscious/aware level and is linked to explicit memory. This system generates emotions more slowly than the other system.

There are specific brain parts involved in these emotion pathways. The limbic system, which is located right above the brain stem, is a control center for the fight or flight responses. The amygdala is particularly involved in fear responses. Recent research indicates that it is also involved in some positive emotions since it acts as a transfer station.

Other brain parts involved in emotion include the reticular formation which acts as an alarm and the cerebral cortex which interprets events and associates them with memories. There is some evidence that the two hemispheres of the brain process different emotions. This is called the lateralization of emotion.

The autonomic nervous system has a role in both types of emotions. The sympathetic nervous system activates in response to unpleasant emotions while the parasympathetic play a role in more pleasant emotions. Many hormones in the endocrine system are associated with specific emotions.

There are several theories of emotion. The James-Lange theory says that people experience physiological changes and then interpret those changes as emotional states. They cry and then they feel sad. We do not experience an emotion until after the body is aroused and responds with physiological changes. Feeling is essence of emotion.

The Cannon-Bard theory says that arousal and emotion occur simultaneously. When we are emotional, the thalamus and cerebral cortex are stimulated simultaneously and thus the emotional feelings accompany physiological changes.

The Schachter-Singer theory, often called the two-factor theory, is a cognitive approach. It incorporates elements of both the James Lange and Cannon Bard theories. People do interpret their bodily changes but it is within a specific context and they then infer emotion from those cues. The cognitive appraisal theory is another cognitive theory. It says that individuals decide on an appropriate emotion following the event. The opponent process theory says that emotions work in pairs. When one is activated, the opponent emotion is suppressed.

How do the theories of emotion explain performance? The inverted-U function says that too much or too little arousal can impair performance. The optimal level of arousal for particular tasks needs to be identified. Martin Zuckerman studied sensation seekers who need high levels of arousal.

How Much Control Do We Have Over Our Emotions?

Core Concept – <u>Although emotional responses are not always consciously regulated, we can learn to control them.</u>

A recent line of research focuses on emotional intelligence which is defined the ability to understand and control emotional responses. Researchers are developing a test, similar to an IQ test, to measure emotional intelligence. It is a variable that psychologists believe can help us understand and predict behavior.

Another area of research related to the study of emotion is deception. Researchers who study deception have found that most people who lie send uncontrolled nonverbal signals of the deception. The polygraph or lie detector is the instrument that attempts to identify when someone is lying. It is based upon the idea that liars exhibit physical signs of arousal. However, both guilty and innocent people may have symptoms of arousal. In addition, it is possible to learn to control or distort emotions. There are serious concerns about the accuracy of the polygraph test.

Motivation: What Makes Us Act as We Do?

Core Concept – <u>Motivation takes many forms but all involved inferred mental processes that select and direct our behavior.</u>

Motivation refers those factors that energize behavior and determine its direction – it comes from the Latin "to move." We think of motivation as any condition (usually internal) that initiates or maintains goal-directed behavior.

Motivation connects observable behavior to internal states. It accounts for variability in behavior and can explain perseverance in the face of adversity. Motives also help us relate biology to behavior.

It is important to distinguish between a motive and a drive. A drive is motivation with a biological component. Motive is used for desires that are learned. Psychologists also distinguish between intrinsic and extrinsic motivation. Intrinsic motivation comes from within and is engaging in an activity for its own sake. Extrinsic motivation comes from outside the person and relates to engaging in an activity for an external reward. Motives can arise from either conscious or unconscious motivation.

There are many theories about why people are motivated to behave as they do. Instinct theory states that humans are born with biologically based behaviors that promote their survival. These instincts do not depend on learning although they can be modified by experience. Because of popular misuse of the term "instinct," ethologists now use the term fixed-action patterns to refer to an unlearned behavior pattern that occurs throughout a species.

The concept of a drive was developed as an alternative to an instinct. Drive theory comes from Clark Hull and is sometimes called Hullian theory. It assumes that we are motivated to act because of a biological need to attain or maintain some goal that helps with the survival of the organism. The ultimate goal is homeostasis or inner stability. This theory does not explain all behavior, though, since not all behavior comes from a basic need or biological drive.

Cognitive theory asserts that people actively determine their own goals and how to achieve those goals. In his social learning theory, Julian Rotter asserted that our motivation is determined by two factors: 1) expectation of attaining a goal and 2) the personal value of the goal. These expectations are governed by our locus of control or belief about our ability to control events. An internal locus of control leads one to believe in control over events while an external locus of control sees outside influences as more important.

Another view of motivation comes from Sigmund Freud's **psychodynamic theory**. Motivation, for Freud, comes mainly from the id in the unconscious mind. He believed that two basic desires that control almost all behavior. The two desires are eros, the desire for sex, and thanatos, the destructive impulse. These desires are not merely instincts. Rather, he sought to explain more complex behaviors.

Abraham Maslow's **humanistic theory** incorporates some of the best elements of the above approaches and brings in the behavioral theories. It emphasizes that life is a totality, not parts and focuses on individual choice and self-worth. He posited a **hierarchy of needs** and said that people are naturally motivated to meet these needs. The levels build one upon another. We must satisfy lower needs before we worry about higher ones. The needs are biological, safety, attachment/affiliation, esteem, and self-actualization. Maslow also raised the importance of social motivation in directing behavior.

We need to examine the issue of culture here. Maslow's theory seems most applicable to people from individualistic cultures. Self-actualization implies that individual development is the pinnacle of motivation. It may not be the highest level in collectivistic cultures. Also, self-actualization can be defined in a variety of ways.

One issue related to motivation is the use of extrinsic rewards. Research has shown that external rewards can diminish intrinsic motivation. This effect is called overjustification.

How Are Achievement, Hunger, and Sex Alike? Different?

Core Concept – <u>Achievement, hunger, and sex exemplify other human motives because they differ not only in the behavior they produce but in the mix of biological, mental, behavioral, and social/cultural influences on them.</u>

The motives discussed in this section are a blend of nature and nurture. They respond differently to internal and environmental cues as well as social and cultural influences. No theorist has been able to develop a theory broad enough to take all of these factors into account. Recent work in evolutionary psychology has suggested that each mechanism evolved in response to a different environmental pressure. However, this theory is not comprehensive and is not a complete explanation for these motives.

The need for achievement is a psychological motive that explains a range of behaviors. Murray and McClelland defined this construct they called n Ach as the desire to attain a difficult but wanted goal. They measure levels of n Ach using a projective measure, the Thematic Apperception Test, in which people respond to ambiguous pictures.

Many psychologists believe that need achievement has strong cultural components. Cultures differ in the value they place on individual achievement. Individualistic cultures such as those common in the Euro-American world place a high value on individual achievements. Collectivist cultures place a higher value on group loyalty and cooperation.

The current view of hunger and eating uses a multiple systems approach. Hunger combines many factors: the body's energy requirements, food preferences, environmental food cues, and cultural demands.

There are clear biological factors involved in hunger as well. Receptors monitor sugar and fat levels and send signals to the lateral hypothalamus which then sends out signals of hunger. An internal scale weighs fat stores; when they fall below a set point, eating behavior is triggered. Pressure detectors in the stomach signal fullness or emptiness. Other mechanisms relate to our preferences for sweet and high-fat food. Physical activity also relates to hunger and fullness.

Eating can also be related to the individual's emotional state. Culture can also influence hunger and eating. Social norms can influence attitudes about body size. Eating disorders are often related to these social norms. Anorexia nervosa is a condition in which an individual weighs less than 85 percent of their normal weight and still worries about being fat. Bulimia is characterized by periods of binging and purging. It can accompany anorexia or be present on its own. While these disorders can be related to social norms, they are present around the world, suggesting other mechanisms contribute. Obesity is another eating disorder.

Thirst can also direct behavior. Volumetric thirst comes from a drop in blood plasma levels. Osmotic thirst results from sweating or losing fluid through the cell walls in other ways.

Unlike other drives, sex is usually a pleasurable drive when aroused. Sexual motivation also serves many other goals including reproduction and social bonding. Culture plays a large role in how people meet these sexual drives.

The first scientific study of sexuality was done by the Kinsey Institute in the mid-twentieth century through interviews. Masters and Johnson in the 1960s and '70s brought the study of sex into the laboratory. They studies the sexual response cycle through observation. They identified four phases of response: excitement, plateau, orgasm, and resolution.

The major sex organ in humans is the brain. Objects become stimuli for arousal through a conditioned association process. Sexual behavior is also governed by sexual scripts which are socially learned programs of sexual responsiveness.

The evolutionary perspective examines sexual motivation and its origination in our genes. The biological goal of both sexes is to have as many offspring as possible. However, the physical costs of reproduction differ for the sexes. Since women can only have a few children over their lifespan, females tend to exhibit caution in mate selection. Males, on the other hand, seek to breed as much as possible. While this evolutionary view can be applied to non-human species, it is not as simple with humans.

While many motives have a biological root, there are also cognitive components to most motivation. One way to examine the cognitive element is to examine the ways in which people resolve conflicts. There are four major ways to think about conflict. Approach-approach is a conflict between two equally attractive options. Approach-avoidance is a conflict in which there are both negative and positive elements to the decision.

Avoidance-avoidance conflicts present two equally unpleasant choices. Multiple approach-avoidance conflicts have many pros and cons on each side and thus are more difficult decisions to make.

There are two forms of sexual orientation: homosexuality and heterosexuality. Sexual orientation refers to the object of one's erotic attraction. It is a complex issue. There are several theories about the origins of sexual orientation. We know that testosterone levels and parenting do not contribute. Research into the biological origins in the brain and genes is promising.

How and Why Do We Experience Stress?

The word stress is used casually in most conversations. Psychologists use the term to mean a physical and mental response to a threatening situation. A stressor is the stimulus that demands adaptation. Adaptation involves both evaluating the stressor and resources for coping. This is known as the process of cognitive appraisal.

Core Concept – The human stress response to perceived threat activates thoughts, feelings, behaviors and physiological arousal that normally promote adaptation and survival.

Historically humans had to deal with primitive stressors such as climate extremes, scarce resources, and hostile neighbors. Starvation was possible. Our ancestors developed the fight or flight response to cope with these difficulties. The same physiological responses continued as learned responses to current stressors, especially loss and catastrophe.

Catastrophic responses qualify as traumatic stressors which arouse fear, horror, or helplessness. Terrorism is a particular traumatic stressor. Researchers have identified five stages of the response to trauma. In order, the stages are psychic numbness, automatic action, communal effort, letdown, and recovery. Such events can also induce posttraumatic stress disorder which includes a delayed stress reaction and involuntary re-experiencing of the trauma.

Stress produces a physiological response that is similar to that our ancestors felt. This response follows the same sequence of events. Initial arousal occurs followed by a protective behavioral reaction. The autonomic nervous system and endocrine systems react and there is a decrease in the effectiveness of the immune system. The basic pattern is the fight or flight response. It occurs in both acute stress, temporary patterns of arousal as well as in chronic stress.

How do these stress reactions and the accompanying negative emotions affect health? Han Selye has identified what he called the general adaptation syndrome. Stress responses can be helpful but when they are prolonged, they can contribute to, but not cause, diseases such as heart disease, ulcers, arthritics, and asthma.

Selye's model includes a three-stage response to stress. The alarm reaction is when the hypothalamus sets off a response through the endocrine system. Adrenal hormones are released and the sympathetic nervous system is activated. In stage 2, resistance, arousal subsides as the parasympathetic system activates and adrenal output slows. The third stage, exhaustion, includes a reappearance of the general arousal of Stage 1 along with a parasympathetic response to counter that arousal. Prolonged exposure to these neurotransmitters and hormones can have a negative impact on health.

Fight or flight is not the only response available. Withdrawal is another possible response. The general inhibition syndrome is likely when one feels helpless. Shelley Taylor has proposed the tend and befriend model of stress response. This model focuses on the female response to stress and posits that females are biologically predisposed to nurture and protect during a threat.

One line of recent research has focused on the impact of stress on the immune system and on cytokines in particular. The field of psychoneuroimmunology focuses on the study of the connections between stress and the body. Other research has looked at personality characteristics and stress. Type A personalities who have hostile tendencies tend to have a higher risk of cardiac disease. Type B personalities have a more relaxed approach to life.

Two other concepts are related to stress. Learned helplessness occurs when an individual develops an attitude of passive resignation as a response to stimuli. Others are examining the concept of resilience and how people can develop resilience.

Sample Multiple Choice

1. You are hiking in the mountains when you unexpectedly encounter a wild dog who bares his teeth at you. Immediately your _____ nervous system kicks into gear.
   A. autonomic
   B. peripheral
   C. somatic
   D. emotional
   E. parasympathetic

2. Your friend believes that there are some emotions that are universally recognized. She is espousing the theory of _____.
   A. Freud
   B. Plutchik
   C. Ekman
   D. Darwin
   E. James

3. When you are in a dangerous situation and you become alert to the possible dangers, your _____ receives messages from the quick and unconscious emotion processing pathway and prepares you to defend yourself.
   A. reticular activating system
   B. hypothalamus
   C. hippocampus
   D. thalamus
   E. amygdala

4. "We feel sorry because we cry" represents the theory of _____.
   A. James-Lange
   B. Cannon- Bard
   C. LeDoux
   D. Schachter
   E. Freud

5. "We cry when we feel sorry" represents the theory of _____.
   A. James- Lange
   B. Cannon- Bard
   C. LeDoux
   D. Schachter
   E. Freud

6. "We cry when we notice we feel sorry inside and are involved in a sad situation" represents the theory of _____.
   A. James- Lange
   B. Cannon- Bard
   C. LeDoux
   D. Schachter
   E. Freud

7. You admit that you like your job but that the main reason that you work is because you get paid every week. Your motivation is primarily _____.
   A. deferred
   B. intrinsic
   C. extrinsic
   D. secondary
   E. primary

8. Someone such as Ghandi or Mother Teresa would reach the _____ level of Maslow's theory of motivation.
   A. safety needs
   B. biological needs
   C. attachment and affiliation
   D. esteem needs
   E. self-actualization

9. Larry is a professional football player who has made millions of dollars playing football. When he first began playing as a child, he loved the game. However, he finds going to the practice field a chore these days. Psychologists would say this is the result of _____.
   A. extrinsic motivation
   B. intrinsic motivation
   C. overjustification effect
   D. talent overload
   E. work overload

10. You scored poorly on your math final because you never did any of the homework problems nor did you study for any of the tests. You blame your failure on yourself because you did not study as you should have. You are exhibiting a(n) _____ locus of control.
    A. essential
    B. natural
    C. internal
    D. external
    E. basic

11. The innate response that occurs when you are threatened or in danger is known as the _____ response.
    A. survival
    B. fear
    C. endurance
    D. stress
    E. fight or flight

12. Sonja's hometown was destroyed by a tornado. While no one was killed, the extensive damage and aftermath caused much _____ stress to the townspeople.
    A. disaster
    B. overwhelming
    C. catastrophic
    D. traumatic
    E. unexpected

13. Phil encounters a difficult question on his calculus final. He rereads the question 5 times and decides that it is impossible. He feels his stress level rising. _____ has led to this increase in stress.
    A. Interpretation
    B. Nervousness
    C. Cognitive appraisal
    D. Cognitive evaluation
    E. Math anxiety

14. Selye's _____ suggests that chronic negative emotional states tend to produce disease-causing changes in the body, unhealthy behavior patterns, and poor personal relationships.
    A. Stress Syndrome
    B. General Adaptation Syndrome
    C. Fight-or-flight response
    D. General Inhibition Syndrome
    E. Alarm reaction

15. _____ is the study of the healing interactions between brain, body, emotions, and the immune system.
    A. Resilience
    B. Stress and coping
    C. Health psychology
    D. Hardiness
    E. Psychoneuroimmunology

Respond to the following question using proper psychological terminology. Remember to define the selected terms and support your answer by referencing the situation posed.

Explain what each of the following is and how each would function in the situation of a person who lived in southern Louisiana during Hurricane Katrina.

  a) amygdala
  b) instinct theory
  c) posttraumatic stress
  d) Schachter's two factor theory
  e) cognitive appraisal

Sample Question Answers

Multiple Choice Answers

1. A is the correct answer. The autonomic nervous system is the routing system for situations when you become emotionally aroused.

2. B is the correct answer. Paul Ekman posits the idea that some emotions are universal.

3. E is the correct answer. The amygdala processes information from the quick and unconscious pathways, particularly with fear.

4. A is the correct answer. The crying, the physical response to a stimuli, comes first and then the emotion of sorrow. This is the James Lange theory.

5. B is the correct answer. The physical response and the feeling occur simultaneously. That is the Cannon Bard theory.

6. D is the correct answer. The Schachter two-factor theory says that emotion results from the cognitive appraisal of the physical arousal and the emotion.

7. C is the correct answer. The primary motivation is extrinsic or outside of the person.

8. E is the correct answer. Self-actualization is the highest level pf the hierarchy of needs. People such as Mother Teresa are at that level.

9. C is the correct answer. The overjustification effect says that when the extrinsic reward becomes too large it can stifle intrinsic motivation.

10. C is the correct answer. You are putting the responsibility on yourself which is an internal locus of control.

11. E is the correct answer. Fight or flight is the name of the inborn response that occurs when we are threatened.

12. D is the correct answer. Traumatic stress is what occurs during a catastrophic event such as a tornado.

13. C is the correct answer. Cognitive appraisal is the identification of a threat and determination of coping skills. It can lead to increased stress when we feel unable to cope.

14. B is the correct answer. Selye called his syndrome the General Adaptation Syndrome.

15. E is the correct answer. Psychoneuroimmunology is the field that examines these interactions.

<u>Free Response Answer</u>
This question would be scored using a rubric. The question has the following points:

Terms – 5 points
Application – 5 points
1. The amygdala initiates fear and avoidance responses.
2. During the hurricane, the amygdala is the part of the brain that would first signal fear as the hurricane approached.

3. Instinct theory is a theory of motivation that says certain behaviors are determined by innate factors.
4. Many of the survival behaviors after the hurricane could be explained by instinct theory.

5. Posttraumatic stress is a delayed stress reaction in which the individual involuntarily re-experiences the trauma.
6. Many of those who lived through Katrina have had episodes of posttraumatic stress disorder.

7. Schachter's two factor theory says that emotion arises from our cognitive appraisal of the physical arousal and of the emotion-provoking stimulus.
8. As people assessed both the danger and their physical arousal, they determined which emotion they would feel. That would also change throughout the course of the Katrina event.

9. Cognitive appraisal is comprised of our perception of a threat and our resources for coping.
10. Many people who lived through Katrina reacted differently. This theory could explain those differences since some felt more able to cope.

Chapter Nine – Psychological Development

How Do Psychologists Explain Development?

Core Concept – <u>Development is a process of growth, change, and consistency brought about by an interaction of heredity and environment.</u>

Developmental psychology is the psychological specialty that studies how organisms change over time as the result of biological and environmental influences. The **nature-nurture issue** is the long-standing discussion over the relative importance of heredity (nature) and the environment (nurture) in their influence on behavior and mental processes. Heredity and environment work through **interaction**, a process by which forces work together or influence each other, in the developmental process.

The contributions of heredity and environment in human development have been studied through twin studies, adoption, studies, and familial studies. **Identical twins** are a pair who started life as a single fertilized egg which later split into two distinct individuals. Identical twins have exactly the same genes. When we look at twins who were adopted by separate families, we can look closely at the issue of nature and nurture. However, twin studies must be interpreted with caution. **Fraternal twins** are a pair who started life as two separate fertilized eggs that shared the same womb. Fraternal twins, on average, have about 50 percent of their genetic material in common. Psychologists study the genetic contributions to psychological traits to determine which traits are solely caused by genetics and which are the result of predispositions.

The question of how children become adults is a continuing debate. The **continuity view** is the perspective that development is gradual and continuous as opposed to the **discontinuity view**, which states that development proceeds in an uneven fashion. This view focuses on development in stages. **Developmental stages** are periods of life initiated by significant transitions or changes in physical or psychological functioning.

What Capabilities Does the Child Possess?

Core Concept – <u>Newborns have innate abilities for finding nourishment, interacting with others, and avoiding harmful situations, while developing abilities of infants or children rely more on learning.</u>

The **prenatal period** is the developmental period before birth. A **zygote** is a fertilized egg. An **embryo** is the name for the developing human organism during the first eight weeks of conception. The **fetus** is the term for the developing human organism between the embryonic stage and birth. The **placenta** is the organ interface between the embryo or fetus and the mother. The placenta separates the bloodstreams, but it allows the exchange of nutrients and waste products. Teratogens are substances from the environment, including viruses, drugs, and other chemicals, that can damage the developing organism during the prenatal period.

The developing brain grows neurons, which originate at the *neural tube*, at the rate of up to 250,000 per minute. The **neonatal period,** or newborn period, extends through the first month after birth. Neonates have remarkable sensory abilities and reflexes including the postural reflex, grasping reflex, and sucking reflex.

Infancy spans the time between the end of the neonatal period and the establishment of language, usually at about eighteen months to two years. All of these abilities come from a nervous system that is developing at a rapid rate. It reaches ultimate mass at age eleven.

Infants experience learning as an aspect of their development. Classical conditioning plays a role in the connection between the world and sensory events. As develop proceeds, learning assumes a large role in producing complex behaviors.

Infant social abilities include forming an **attachment**, an enduring social-emotional relationship between a child and a parent or other regular caregiver. Konrad Lorenz pioneered the study of **imprinting,** which is a primitive form of learning in which some young animals follow and form an attachment to the first moving object they see and hear. Mary Ainsworth studied attachment styles using the Strange Situation Test. She identified three styles of attaching: secure, insecure, and avoidant.

Harry and Margaret Harlow studied attachment in monkeys. The Harlows concluded that the **contact comfort,** stimulation, and reassurance derived from the physical touch of a caregiver that mothers provide is essential for normal social development. Without this contact, psychosocial dwarfism or failure to thrive may occur.

Maturation is the process by which the genetic program manifests itself over time. Most infants follow a predetermined sequence of development. However, it is the interaction of biology and environment that is most important. Most development is continuous although much physical growth occurs in spurts. Developmental psychologists call this sudden physical growth saltation, a Latin word which means leap.

What are the Developmental Tasks of Infancy and Childhood?

Core Concept – Infants and children face especially important developmental tasks in the areas of cognition and social relationships – tasks that lay a foundation fro further growth in adolescence and adulthood.

Jean Piaget studied children's cognitive development. Piaget's theory contains three key ideas: schema, assimilation and accommodation, and stages of cognitive development. **Schemas** are the mental structures or programs that guide a developing child's thought. **Assimilation** is a mental process that modifies new information to fit into existing schemas. **Accommodation** is a mental process that restructures existing schemes so that new information is better understood.

Piaget's stage theory of cognitive development explains how children progress through the sensorimotor, preoperational, concrete operational, and formal operational stages. The **sensorimotor stage** is from birth to about age two, during which the child relies heavily on motor responses to stimuli. Key tasks during the sensorimotor stage include **mental representation** (the ability to form internal images of objects and events) and **object permanence** (the knowledge that an object exists independently of one's own actions or awareness).

The **preoperational stage** lasts from about two years of age to about six or seven years of age. It is characterized by use of language and well-developed mental representations. Characteristics of a child's mind during the preoperational stage include **egocentrism** (the self-centered inability to realize that there are other viewpoints besides one's own), **animistic thinking** (inanimate objects are imagined to have life and mental processes), **centration** (inability to consider more than one factor at a time), and **irreversibility** (the inability to think through a series of events or mental operations and then mentally reverse the steps).

The **concrete operational stage** occurs from about seven years of age until about eleven years of age and is characterized by understanding **conservation** (physical properties of an object or substance do not change when appearances change but nothing is added or taken away) and the acquisition of **mental operations** (solving problems by manipulating images in one's mind). A child in the concrete operational stage is still incapable of abstract thought. The **formal operational** stage occurs from about age eleven onward, and is characterized by abstract thought and reasoning. Piaget's theories are sometimes criticized for not considering the transitions between stages as continuous.

Social and emotional development includes a **theory of mind**, which is an awareness that other people's behavior may be influenced by beliefs, desires, and emotions that differ from one's own. It is also a set of expectations about how people behave in specific situations. It is fundamental to social interaction.

Jerome Kagan researched children's **temperament**, the characteristic manner of behavior or reaction that is assumed to have a strong genetic basis. While temperament can be identified in infants, it can be modified by both experience and parenting.

Lev Vygotsky emphasized the importance of social relationships in a child's cognitive development. The **zone of proximal development** refers to the difference between what a child can do with help and what the child can do without any help or guidance. Vygotsky saw socialization as a lifelong process that is shaped by influences in a child's life.

Parenting style is one of those influences. Parenting styles differ, and they can contribute to a child's development. Authoritative parenting is very effective and means that a parent is warm, attentive, and sensitive to a child's needs and interests. Authoritarian parenting is frequently degrading, cold, and rejecting. Permissive parenting is indulgent and warm, but is not the most effective for healthy development. The uninvolved parent is emotionally detached, withdrawn, and inattentive.

The role of daycare in development raises important questions. The research is mixed. Most children do very well in daycare. However, the quality of the childcare is the most important aspect of its impact on development.

Development is also influenced by participation in school and leisure activities and gender differences. Erik Erikson explored development as a series of **psychosocial stages**. These eight developmental stages refer to major challenges that appear successively across the lifespan. An individual must rethink one's relationships and goals at each stage. Childhood stages include resolving issues of trust vs. mistrust, autonomy vs. self-doubt, initiative vs. guilt, and competence vs. inferiority. Criticisms of Erikson's theory include the lack of scientific basis as it was based solely on clinical observation, and an inaccurate representation of women's development.

What Changes Mark the Transition of Adolescence?

Core Concept – Adolescence offers new developmental challenges growing out of physical changes, cognitive changes, and socioeconomic pressures.

In industrialized societies, **adolescence** is a developmental period beginning at puberty and ending at adulthood. **Rites of passage** are social rituals that mark the transition between developmental stages, especially between childhood and adulthood. These rites vary widely among cultures. Our own culture has few rituals to help children make this transition.

Approaching adolescence is marked by the pubescent growth spurt. Physical maturation begins with the onset of **puberty,** the onset of sexual maturity. The **primary sex characteristics**, the sex organs and genitals, undergo dramatic change as secondary sex characteristics which are gender related physical features that emerge during puberty. These secondary characteristics are pubic hair, facial hair, and deepening voice in males and pubic hair, widened hips, and enlarged breasts in females. Body image becomes especially important in the teenage years.

Cognitively, adolescents are in Piaget's **formal operational stage**. During this time, the capacity for abstract and complex thought develops. Hormonal changes and the growth of the frontal lobes of the brain contribute to the cognitive changes of adolescence. An increase in sensation-seeking and risk-taking is common.

According to Erikson, during the "identity crisis," adolescents must define their identities as individuals even as they seek the comfort and feeling of belonging that comes from being with family and friends. Some adolescents experiment with different norms- such as clothing or hairstyles- within the security of supportive relationships with companions, cliques, or romantic partners. Is adolescence a period of turmoil? While some adolescents have conflicts, research does not support the stereotype of adolescence as a period of overwhelming turmoil.

Sexual issues are very important in adolescence. One issue that arises for most adolescents is sexual orientation. Overwhelmingly adolescents are heterosexual. There is evidence that males and females differ in their initial sexual experiences. For females, emotional involvement is more important than is for males.

Lawrence Kohlberg developed a widely studied theory of moral development. He studied how people's moral thinking was elicited when they were faced with moral dilemmas. Stage 1 is preconventional moral thinking that is motivated by pain avoidance or fear of being caught. Conventional morality involves gaining acceptance, avoiding disapproval, following rules, and avoiding penalties. Postconventional morality promotes the welfare of one's society, achieving justice, being consistent with one's principles, and avoiding self-condemnation. Moral development appears culturally consistent. Carol Gilligan criticized the male bias in Kohlberg's theory.

What Developmental Challenges Do Adults Face?

Core Concept – Nature and nurture continue to produce changes throughout life, but in adulthood, these changes include both growth and decline.

According to Erikson, young adulthood poses the challenge of establishing close relationships during the stage he labeled as intimacy vs. isolation. Anything that isolates from social supports puts us at risk for illness. During midlife, Erikson identifies, **generativity** (a process of making a commitment beyond one's self to family, work, society, or future generations) versus stagnation, as the major conflict that must be overcome. Erikson identifies the "ego-integrity vs. despair" stage as one in which older adults must evaluate life choices.

Older adults who pursue high levels of environmental stimulation tend to maintain higher levels of cognitive abilities. They face diminished vision and hearing in many cases. While some parts of the brain lose mass, most older adults do not have a decrease in cognitive abilities. **Alzheimer's disease**—a degenerative brain disease usually noticed by its debilitating effects on memory—is a concern, however. A problem for older adults can be **selective social interaction**, choosing to restrict the number of one's social contacts to those who are most gratifying.

Elisabeth Kubler-Ross identified five stages of death and dying. These stages are **denial**, **anger, bargaining, depression,** and finally **acceptance.** While her early writings claimed that these stages were invariable, later research has shown the sequence is individual.

<u>**Sample Multiple Choice**</u>

1. The correct order of prenatal development is _____.
   A. zygote, fetus, embryo
   B. zygote, embryo, fetus
   C. fetus, embryo, zygote
   D. embryo, fetus zygote
   E. embryo, zygote, fetus

2. Now that Sally is six years old, she is better able to empathize with her friend's feeling than she did when she was three years old. Sally is acquiring a(n) _____.
   A. self-concept
   B. schema
   C. temperament
   D. theory of mind
   E. assimilation

3. What is the main reason a child can be born addicted to drugs?
   A. The mother uses drugs and it crosses the placenta into the child's bloodstream.
   B. The hereditary trait for addiction in manifested in utero.
   C. The fetus' chromosomes are not fully developed until birth.
   D. Personality traits, such as addiction, are evident at birth.
   E. A child is not capable of being born addicted to drugs.

4. In Piaget's concrete operational stage, a child acquires an understanding of the principle of _____.
   A. conservation
   B. abstract thinking
   C. attachment
   D. object permanence
   E. separation anxiety

5. According to Piaget, egocentrism is most characteristic of the _____ stage of cognitive development.
   A. sensorimotor
   B. preoperational
   C. concrete operational
   D. formal operational
   E. assimilation

6. The Harlow studies of attachment in monkeys concluded that _____.
   A. food was the monkeys' greatest motivator
   B. contact was preferred by the monkeys
   C. loneliness was experienced by monkeys that were without playmates
   D. imprinting matters more than attachment
   E. the temperature of the test rooms was the most important variable

7. In preconventional morality, a person behaves based on _____.
   A. a sense of moral obligation
   B. gaining social approval
   C. avoiding punishment
   D. the universal good of humanity
   E. obeying the laws

8. Maria is able to think logically about abstract themes in her novel. According to Piaget, Maria is in the _____ stage.
   A. preoperational thought
   B. concrete operations
   C. formal operations
   D. sensorimotor thought
   E. animistic thought

9. Mrs. Lee is an elderly woman who reflects on her life with satisfaction and joy. According to Erikson, Mrs. Lee has reached the_____ stage of development.
   A. generavity
   B. isolation
   C. intimacy
   D. acceptance
   E. integrity

10. The Ramos family is very close. Mr. and Mrs. Ramos are very warm people who support their children and discuss clear expectations and concerns in a non-judgmental manner. Jack and Annie Ramos are their children who are very responsible and happy young people. What type of parenting do Mr. and Mrs. Ramos probably practice?
    A. Neglectful
    B. Authoritarian
    C. Authoritative
    D. Indulgent
    E. Indifferent

11. According to Erikson, _____ is a key task of adolescence.
    A. experimenting with sex and drugs
    B. searching for identity
    C. learning to reason abstractly
    D. establishing intimacy
    E. experiencing generativity

12. Donna, a junior in high school, joins the student government because all of her friends and family think that she should. Donna is at the _____ stage of moral reasoning.
    A. preconventional
    B. conventional
    C. postconventional
    D. formal
    E. concrete

13. In the nature-nurture debate, to which of the following does the "nurture" refer?
    A. Critical periods
    B. Imprinting
    C. Environmental factors
    D. Hereditary factors
    E. Traits

14. Konrad Lorenz's work illustrated the strength of _____.
    A. conservation
    B. language acquisition
    C. imprinting
    D. assimilation
    E. accommodation

15. Danny understands that a tall beaker and a short beaker hold the same amount of water. Danny is demonstrating an understanding of _____.
    A. object permanence
    B. conservation
    C. assimilation
    D. accommodation
    E. critical periods

Sample Free Response Question

Respond to the following question using proper psychological terminology. Remember to define the selected terms and support your answer by referencing it to the situation posed.

Danny and Brian are twins. Explain how each of the following may affect their development.
    a) identical twins
    b) schema
    c) animism
    d) zone of proximal development
    e) attachment theory

Sample Question Answers

Multiple Choice Questions

1. B is the correct answer. Prenatal development is divided into the following stages: zygote, embryo, fetus.

2. D is the correct answer. A theory of mind involves awareness of others' behaviors and feelings.

3. A is the correct answer. Drugs are teratogens that cross the placenta.

4. A is the correct answer. Understanding of the principle of conservation is acquired during the concrete operations stage.

5. B is the correct answer. Egocentrism is characteristic of the preoperational stage.

6. B is the correct answer. The Harlow studies demonstrated the importance of physical contact in forming attachments.

7. C is the correct answer. Avoiding punishment is characteristic of preconventional moral development.

8. D is the correct answer. Abstract thinking is characteristic of the formal operational stage of cognitive development.

9. E is the correct answer. In late adulthood integrity is a sense of life satisfaction.

10. C is the correct answer. Authoritative parenting is effective and brings results in secure children. (Hint: remember that authoritative ends in "ve" for very effective, this will help avoid the confusion with authoritarian parenting.)

11. B is the correct answer. Resolving an identity crisis is a key adolescent task.

12. B is the correct answer. At the conventional level of moral reasoning we do things that meet the expectations of others.

13. C is the correct answer. Environmental factors are the nurture aspect of the nature-nurture controversy.

14. C is the correct answer. Lorenz's work illustrated the concept of imprinting.

15. B is the correct answer. He understands that a change in physical form does not change physical properties

Free Response Answer
This answer will be scored using a rubric. The question has the following points:

Terms – 5 points
Applications -5 points

1) Identical twins are a pair that develop from a single fertilized egg that later splits.
2) Identical twins have the exact same genes and share many similarities.

3) Schema is a basic framework of ideas about ideas, things, and people based on experience.
4) As the twins develop, the principles of assimilation and accommodation will alter their schemas.

5) Animism is the belief that inanimate objects are living.
6) The preoperational child may think that the "chair is crying." The twins may not develop this characteristic as the same time.

7) Zone of Proximal Development is the range between what a child can do alone and what a child can do with the help of skilled helpers.
8) Danny and Brian will write more neatly when a teacher instructs them in handwriting.

9) Attachment Theory examines the close emotional bond between children and caregivers.
10) Danny and Brian are securely attached children who are socially competent children.

Chapter Ten – Personality

What Forces Shape Our Personalities?

Core Concept – <u>According to the psychodynamic, humanistic, and cognitive theories, personality is a continuously changing process, shaped by our internal needs and cognitions and by external pressures from the social environment.</u>

Personality is those reasonably stable patterns of behavior, thought, and emotion that distinguish one person from another. There are many approaches to understanding personality. These approaches are particularly important to clinical psychologists since the explanations for and treatments of disorders are linked to personality theory. Yet there is little universal agreement among psychologists about what personality is and how to measure it.

Approaches to personality can be divided into three groups—three perspectives that describe personality as dynamic and developing. They each emphasize the interplay of mental processes and social interaction. Each, however, emphasizes a different combination of these factors.

There are several psychodynamic approaches to understanding personality and each is slightly different but there are some common cores. Each says personality is a dynamic struggle, a theory based on conflict between inner drives control and direct behavior.

Psychoanalysis is the approach associated with Freud. He saw personality as three levels: preconscious, conscious, and unconscious. The unconscious urges are kept below the surface by repression and other defense mechanisms. The unconscious is at the center of the personality. Energy comes in two forces. Eros is passionate love and is guided by the **libido**. Thanatos is the death instinct.

The personality has three structures: **id, ego,** and **superego**. The id is the unconscious storehouse of basic motives and instinctive drives. The id follows the pleasure principle. The superego is guided by moral principle and is analogous to the conscience. The ego has to satisfy the demands of the id without offending the superego. The ego is guided by the reality principle.

Freud posited five stages of psychosexual development: oral, anal, phallic, latency, and genital. Childhood is most the most critical time in development. Boys may develop an **Oedipus complex** or an erotic attraction for their mothers. They displace their attraction to females and develop an **identification** with their fathers. Girls develop **penis envy**.

Freud saw difficulties early in life as leading to **fixation** or arrested psychological development. One way the ego copes is by developing **ego defense mechanisms**. **Repression** excludes unacceptable thought and feelings from awareness. Other important defense mechanisms include denial, rationalization, reaction formation, displacement, regression, sublimation, and projection.

Projective tests are used to measure personality in psychoanalytic theory. There no clear and specified answers. The instrument is composed of ambiguous pictures and figures. People are assumed to project personality into their responses. Two of the most common projective tests are the **Rorschach inkblot technique** and the Thematic Apperception Test (TAT).

For a Freudian, everything a person does is important. **Psychic determinism** refers to the facts that all of our behavior is determined by unconscious processes involving some sort of conflict.

Freud's was the first comprehensive theory of personality. He has had a wide-ranging influence on the study of personality and abnormality. Critics claim that many of Freud's ideas are not testable and that the theory is a poor predictor of future behavior. Additionally, critics say that Freud's views of women are wrong. Others say that the unconscious mind is not as smart or purposeful as Freud believed. There are also the **neo-Freudians** who retained many of his basic ideas but disagreed about the specific motives that underlie personality.

Carl Jung helped Freud refine the psychoanalytic theory but later split with him over some theoretical differences. Jung said that sexual instinct is only one motive and believed there are others that guide our behavior. He said we have a **personal unconscious** which was similar to Freud's id but we also have a **collective unconscious** that holds universal archetypes and memories. Among these archetypes are the anima (female) and animus (male). Everyone possesses both.

His principle of opposites depicts personality as opposing pairs. Our overall pattern is our personality type. One of the most famous pairs is introversion and extraversion. Jung's work is the basis for the Myers-Briggs Type indicator.

Karen Horney and Anna Freud are the two most prominent female psychoanalysts. Horney disputed the concepts of the Oedipus complex and penis envy. For her, normal growth involved social relationships. Development could be blocked by basic anxiety. Unhealthy development involves ten neurotic needs which are normal desires taken to extremes.

Alfred Adler proposed theories focuses on birth order and the **inferiority complex** which he saw as largely unconscious. Out of the complex comes the idea of **compensation** in which the individual tries to make up for deficiencies.

Other neo-Freudians espoused the ideas of unconscious motivation and psychic determinism but differed from Freud on the details. The most important changes include a greater emphasis on ego functions, importance of social variables and the continued development of personality beyond childhood.

The humanistic theories focus more on the normal personality. They are optimistic about human nature. There is more focus on conscious, subjective experience. People are free and responsible for their own behavior and they can make authentic choices.

Gordon Allport was one of the first humanistic theorists with his trait/dispositional theory. Individuals have three types of traits: central, secondary, and cardinal. **Central traits** form the core of personality. **Secondary traits** are attitudes and preferences while **cardinal traits** define people's lives.

Abraham Maslow saw humanism as the "third force" in psychology. He argued for a theory that focuses on mental health. He developed his hierarchy of needs from his study of **self-actualizing personalities** who are people he saw pursuing higher ideals.

Carl Rogers examined the fully functioning person who has a self-concept that is positive and congruent. He insisted on including the reality of perceptions and feelings which he terms the **phenomenal field**. He said we each have subjective experience which colors our perceptions and our sense of self, similar to the Freudian's ego. Rogers believes that everyone has the capacity for growth if we receive unconditional positive regard.

While the humanistic approach was a welcome change, there are criticisms of this theory. Many of the concepts are seen as fuzzy and many cannot be tested. Cross-cultural psychologists criticize the emphasis on self as not relevant to their culture. The recent movement, **positive psychology**, has many of the same goals as the humanistic approach.

The cognitive theorists built on an emphasis on research. They are not as comprehensive as the humanistic or psychodynamic theorists. This approach examines specific influences on personality. Albert Bandura said that our expectations of how we affect others drive us. Humans can foresee the consequences of behavior. **Observational learning** is an important component. Cognitions are also important and come from the interaction with the environment. He called this **reciprocal determinism**.

Julian Rotter is another cognitive theorist. He said the way our behavior functions is related to our sense of personal power or locus of control. An internal locus means a person believes he or she has control over their lives while an external locus gives credit to outside sources.

Critics of cognitive theory say that the theory puts an overemphasis on rational information processing and that it ignores emotion and the unconscious. Recent cognitivists have incorporated these concepts into their theories. The strength of the theory lies in its solid research base.

Current trends in personality theory have become more eclectic, incorporating elements from many theories. Three important trends include family systems theory, the awareness of cultural differences, and an appreciation of gender influences.

What Persistent Patterns Are Found in Personality?

Historically personality was thought to result from the four humors or fluids in the body. Classification of personality has been an ongoing search. Other terms have included temperament, trait, and type.

Core Concept – <u>Another approach describes personality in terms of stable patterns known as temperaments, traits, and types.</u>

Temperament is defined as the inherited personality dispositions that become apparent in early childhood. Biological dispositions affect our personalities. Neurotransmitters do play a role with some disorders. Temperament does not determine personality but is a contributing factor.

Trait theories see personality as a composite of traits. The **Five-Factor Theory** sees five traits that are important. These traits are openness to experience, conscientiousness, extraversion, agreeableness, and neuroticism. This theory simplified earlier theories related to traits. Critics debate the details in the theory. It appears to have validity across culture. Cattell advanced a theory in which he proposed sixteen major factors.

Trait theories can be measured by numerous tests. The **MMPI-2** is one of the best known. It is exemplary due to its **reliability** or consistency and its validity. **Validity** means the test measures what it claims to measure. Another well-known test is the **Myers-Briggs Type Indicator**. A **type** refers to clusters of trait that are central to personality and are found in many people.

These theories give us the ability to predict behavior in some situations. Critics focus on the "snapshot" nature of personality that comes from these theories. There is also the problem of the self-fulfilling prophecy.

The **person-situation controversy** has come from the cognitive psychologist Walter Mischel. Mischel argued that the situation is more important in determining behavior that knowing a person's traits. His ideas challenge the foundations of personality theory.

What "Theories" Do People Use to Understand Each Other?

Core Concept – <u>People everywhere develop implicit assumptions ("folk theories") about personality but these assumptions vary in important ways across cultures.</u>

Implicit personality theories are our personal explanations of how people's qualities influence their behavior. These theories rely on naïve assumptions. The **fundamental attribution error** is often use. The FAE makes the assumption that undesirable behavior is the result of a personality flaw rather than the situation.

How does culture impact personality? The concept of personality is a Western invention. Many differences are related to the differences between individualistic and collectivist cultures. Other cultural differences that have been identified include: status of age groups, romantic love, stoicism and locus of control The distinction between thinking and feeling also relates to culture.

Sample Multiple Choice

1. The major goal of trait and type personality theories is to _____.
   A. describe current personality characteristics
   B. explain abnormal behavior in a person
   C. create a test to evaluate personality
   D. predict future behavior of individuals
   E. explain normal behavior in a person

2. Jackson believes that the root of all behavior comes from forces in his unconscious. He is a proponent of the _____ theory of personality.
   A. cognitive
   B. social-cognitive
   C. psychodynamic
   D. humanistic
   E. trait

3. Karla went to the grocery store to purchase food for a special dinner. The clerk gave her change for a twenty dollar bill instead of a ten dollar bill. When Karla decided to return the extra change, a Freudian would say her _____ was functioning.
   A. conscious
   B. character
   C. id
   D. ego
   E. superego

4. Miles is very rigid about how everything in his schedule works. His desk must be perfectly arranged, and he gets upset if anything upsets his schedule. Freud would say that Miles has a(n) _____ stage fixation.
   A. oral
   B. anal
   C. phallic
   D. genital
   E. latent

5. Sheldon was stopped by the police for running a red light and he received a ticket which will cost him $100. After he got home and looked at the ticket, he kicked his car's tires several times. Sheldon is using the defense mechanism of _____.
   A. rationalization
   B. sublimation
   C. denial
   D. displacement
   E. regression

6. Abraham Maslow's theory focuses on a lifelong process of striving to realize one's potential that is known as _____.
   A. humanism
   B. self-actualization
   C. sublimation
   D. potential selfism
   E. psychic determinism

7. Rachel's therapist believes that her relationship with her client and her acceptance of Rachel are the most important components of therapy. This reflects the view of the _____ approach to therapy.
   A. client-centered
   B. psychodynamic
   B. behavioral
   C. cognitive
   D. trait

8. Angela works hard to earn high marks on her papers and exams. Rotter would say that Angela has a(n) _____ locus of control.
   A. developed
   B. negative
   C. external
   D. positive
   E. internal

9. Mariellen is very dependable and exercises caution and prudence when making decisions. According to the Five-Factor theory, Mariellen is strong in _____.
   A. openness to experience
   B. conscientiousness
   C. agreeableness
   D. extraversion
   E. neuroticism

10. A test that measures what it says it measures is said to have _____.
    A. validity
    B. consistency
    C. reliability
    D. truth
    E. precision

11. Jack seems to be very conscientious at work, but he often is lackadaisical at home and fails to complete his chores. Whose theory would best explain his personality?
    A. Freud
    B. Maslow
    C. Mischel
    D. Horney
    E. Jung

12. Implicit theories of personality are sometimes called _____ theories.
    A. false
    B. undeveloped
    C. immature
    D. folk
    E. artificial

13. Your theater professor dresses in a style that you consider to be reminiscent of the hippies from the 1970s. Because of the way she dresses, you assume she must be liberal in her politics. This is an example of _____.
    A. an internal locus of control
    B. an implicit personality theory
    C. the fundamental attribution error
    D. self-serving bias
    E. the stereotyping personality error

14. Carl Jung extended the unconscious. He believed that images called _____ helped to govern our behavior.
    A. archetypes
    B. icon
    C. symbol
    D. emblems
    E. pictograms

15. Karen Horney believed that when people feel anxious and unsafe, development is thwarted. The signs of this are exhibited in ten _____ needs.
    A. disenchanted
    B. neurotic
    C. phobic
    D. irrational
    E. fixated

Sample Free Response Question

Respond to the following question using proper psychological terminology. Remember to define the terms and support your answer by referencing it to the situation posed.

Samantha has been acting out in school. She gets into fights and is failing many of her classes. Her parents are in the middle of a divorce and she is shuttling between their houses. What is each of these? How would each of the following apply to her behavior?

        a) id
        b) locus of control
        c) trait theory
        d) displacement
        e) humanistic theory

Sample Question Answers

Multiple Choice Questions

1. A is the correct answer. Trait theories attempt to identify personality characteristics or traits.

2. C is the correct answer. At the heart of psychodynamic theories is the role of the unconscious.

3. E is the correct answer. The superego is the part of the personality that acts as the "conscience."

4. B is the correct answer. Being stuck in the anal stage often results in excessive cleanliness and neatness.

5. D is the correct answer. With the defense mechanism of displacement, we shift the reaction from the actual source to a safer source.

6. B is the correct answer. For Maslow, self-actualization is what we are striving to achieve.

7. A is the correct answer. In client-centered theory, unconditional positive regard is at the core of the therapeutic relationship.

8. E is the correct answer. Someone with an internal locus of control believes that hard work will result in success.

9. B is the correct answer. Conscientiousness is the Five-Factor trait that includes dependability and cautiousness.

10. A is the correct answer. Validity is the characteristic of a test that involves the test measuring what it purports to measure.

11. C is the correct answer. Mischel was the proponent of the person-situation theory which says that the situation is more important that innate characteristics.

12. D. is the correct answer. Implicit personality theories are often called folk theories.

13. C is the correct answer. With the fundamental attribution error we assume the undesirable behavior is related to a personality flaw rather than the situation.

14. A is the correct answer. Jung believed archetypes were ancient memories that reside in the collective unconscious.

15. B is the correct answer. Horney said there are ten neurotic needs that are normal desires taken to extremes that are signs of unhealthy development.

Free Response Answer
This answer will be scored using a rubric. The question has the following points:

Terms – 5 points
Application – 5 points

D. displacement
E. humanistic theory

1) The id is the element in the unconscious in psychodynamic theory that control negative impulses.
2) A psychoanalyst would say that Samantha's id is making her behave in aggressive ways.

3) In Rotter's theory the locus of control determine whether we think we control our behavior or it is controlled by outside forces.
4) Samantha would have an external locus of control as she is letting outside circumstance control her behavior.

5) Trait theory says that our personality is the sum of a series of characteristics.
6) Samantha is exhibiting negative traits.

7) Displacement is one of Freud's defense mechanisms in which anger is put onto a safe source, rather than on the true source.
8) Samantha is displacing her anger at her parents onto schoolmates.

9) Humanistic theory says we are all striving to reach our potential and need unconditional positive regard to do so.
10) Samantha is not working to her potential because she does not feel valued by her parents.

Chapter Eleven – Testing and Individual Differences

How Do We Measure Individual Differences?

Core Concept – Measuring individual differences is an essential component of psychology, but strict guidelines and ethical standards must be followed to ensure results and conclusions are valid and appropriate.

Validity and reliability are essential characteristics of tests used to measure individual differences. **Validity** occurs when a test measures what it purports to measure. **Reliability** means that a test will yield the same results when taken multiple times over time. Validity and reliability are measured in several ways. **Face validity** measures whether a test looks like it tests what it is supposed to test. **Content validity** means the each test item is representative of the larger body of knowledge about the subject that the test covers.

An **item analysis** of each question is done to specifically examine how a test is related to the learning objectives. **Criterion validity** means that the performance of the test taker is measured against a specific learning goal. **Split-half reliability** is a measure of reliability in which a test is split into two parts and an individual's scores on both parts are compared. **Test-retest reliability** means that people get about the same score when they take the test more than once.

Test *standardization* means that the test administration and scoring guidelines are the same for each student and that the test results can be used to draw conclusions about the test takers with respect to the test objectives.

Results among test takers can be compared using the normal distribution. Scores falling near the middle of a normal distribution are in the **normal range**. Extreme ends of the distribution of intelligence tests fall in the mentally retarded range (below 70) or the gifted range (above 130).

There are two types of tests. **Objective tests** can be scored easily by machine and **subjective tests** are those tests where an individual is given an ambiguous figure or an open-ended situation and asked to describe what they see or finish a story. With subjective testing, **inter-rater reliability**, a measure of how similarly two different test scorers would score the same test, is extremely important. In all testing, results need to be properly and appropriately reported and interpreted to the test takers and to other interested parties such as colleges.

How Is Intelligence Measured?

Core Concept – Intelligence testing has a history of controversy, but most psychologists now view intelligence as a normally distributed trait that can be measured by performance on a variety of tasks—both verbal and nonverbal.

Simon and Binet developed a school abilities test for French schoolchildren that measured the child's **mental age** (the average age at which normal, average, individuals achieve a certain score) and **chronological age** (the number of years since the individual's birth). American psychologists borrowed from the Binet-Simon test of school abilities and changed it into the Stanford-Binet test or what we now call the IQ test. This IQ test was used in the assessment of army recruits, immigrants, and schoolchildren.

The **intelligence quotient** is the numerical score on an intelligence test, originally computed by dividing the person's mental age by chronological age and multiplying that number by 100. Problems with the calculation of the IQ formula led to modifications in scoring. Today, IQ is most commonly measured with the *Wechsler Test* (WAIS, WISC, or WPPSI).

Mental retardation often represents the lower 2 percent of the IQ range (about 70) and considers the individual's level of social functioning and other abilities. Causes of mental retardation can be genetic (Down syndrome), environmental (Fetal Alcohol Syndrome), deprivation or neglect, or other unknown causes. Early intervention programs help many mentally retarded children. Giftedness often represents the upper 2 percent of the IQ range (above 130) . **Savant syndrome** is found in individuals who have a remarkable talent in one area even though they are mentally slow in other domains.

What Are the Components of Intelligence?

Core Concept – <u>Some psychologists believe that the essence of intelligence is a single, general factor, while others believe that intelligence is best described as a collection of distinct abilities.</u>

Psychometric theories of intelligence include Spearman's **g factor**, which is a general ability underlying all intelligent mental activity. Raymond Cattell determined that intelligence is broken down into two independent components called **crystallized intelligence** (the knowledge a person has acquired, plus the ability to access that knowledge) and **fluid intelligence** (the ability to see complex relationships and solve problems).

Cognitive theories of intelligence include Sternberg's Triarchic theory and Gardner's multiple intelligences theory. Sternberg's **triarchic theory of intelligence** combines three separate components: **practical intelligence** (the ability to cope with the environment), **analytical intelligence** (the ability to analyze problems), and **creative intelligence** (allows people to see new relationships among concepts). Howard Gardner's theory of multiple intelligences proposes that there are seven (or more) forms of intelligence including linguistic, logical-mathematical, spatial, musical, bodily-kinesthetic, interpersonal, and intrapersonal intelligence.

Definitions of intelligence can vary by culture. One other issue with the use of intelligence tests is the self-fulfilling prophecy. The **self-fulfilling prophecy** is observations or behaviors that result primarily from expectations. Thus, negative expectations based on test scores may come to fruition.

How Do Psychologists Explain IQ Differences among Groups?

Core Concept – While most psychologists agree that both heredity and environment affect intelligence; they disagree on the source of IQ differences among racial and social groups.

The source of intelligence is a continuing debate. Neither environment nor heredity explains the source fully. Intelligence is influenced by heredity as shown by the similar IQ scores of identical twins. The evidence for environmental influences is also persuasive. A nurturing environment has been shown to contribute to intelligence scores.

Heritability refers to the amount of variation within a group raised under the same conditions that can be attributed to genetic differences. Heritability tells nothing about between-group differences. We only talk about heritability if we are talking about groups raised in the same environment. We do not talk about individual differences when we talk about heritability.

The Jensen controversy revolved around his thesis that the differences in racial IQ scores are genetically based. In response, many psychologists have identified environmental factors that could contribute to the racial differences in IQ scores. The Scarr and Weinberg adoption study results illustrate the strength of environment in IQ scores.

Social class affects IQ in terms of nutrition, health care, and education. Head Start is an early intervention program that provides an enriched environment for disadvantaged children. Test biases can also influence IQ scores. Many other variables influence differences in IQ scores. Extreme views such as **eugenics** (a philosophy and political movement that encouraged biologically superior people to interbreed and discourage biologically inferior people from having offspring) have emerged and have been used by some to justify their racism.

Sample Multiple Choice

1. A test that measures what it purports to measure is said to have _____.
    A. internal consistency
    B. reliability
    C. validity
    D. aptitude
    E. achievement

2. A test has yielded the same pass rates in 2000, 2001, 2002, 2003, 2004, 2005, 2006. This indicates that the test is probably _____.
    A. internally consistent
    B. reliable
    C. valid
    D. highly aptitude predictable
    E. externally consistent

3. Maria scored 9/10 in part one of her test and 9/10 in part two of her test. Maria's test demonstrates _____.
   A. high achievement indication
   B. face validity
   C. content validity
   D. split half reliability
   E. test retest reliability

4. A multiple-choice test is an example of a(n)_____ test.
   A. aptitude
   B. achievement
   C. objective
   D. subjective
   E. biased

5. When a subjective test is given, _____ is a critical component in determining the test's reliability and validity.
   A. face validity
   B. content validity
   C. inter-rater reliability
   D. split half reliability
   E. item analysis

6. The original purpose of Alfred Binet's intelligence test was to _____.
   A. identify schoolchildren who needed academic support
   B. identify the best military leaders
   C. limit the number of immigrants entering the United States
   D. determine entry into elite universities
   E. prove that genetics was the most important factor in determining the level of an individual's intelligence

7. A six-year-old has a mental age of nine-year-old. What is this child's IQ?
   A. 69
   B. 100
   C. 125
   D. 150
   E. 66

8. Tiffany has an IQ of 56. Which of the following is probably true?
   A. The test was invalid.
   B. Tiffany is mentally retarded.
   C. Tiffany is academically gifted.
   D. Tiffany is a savant.
   E. Tiffany has an identical twin.

9. Tony has an IQ of 60, but he can accurately tell you the date of every upcoming Tuesday throughout the next century. Tony can best be described as _____.
   A. academically gifted
   B. autistic
   C. savant
   D. incapable of self-care
   E. linguistically intelligent

10. Spearman's term for the generalized body of knowledge that underlies intelligence is called _____ intelligence.
   A. spatial
   B. linguistic
   C. g factor
   D. fluid
   E. crystallized

11. According to Howard Gardener, an athlete would most likely demonstrate _____ intelligence.
   A. interpersonal
   B. kinesthetic
   C. spatial
   D. intrapersonal
   E. linguistic

12. Jane convinces herself that she is a poor math student, and even though she studied for the test, she still failed and says to her friend "See, I told you I was a poor math student!" This situation best illustrates the concept of _____.
   A. gender bias
   B. self-fulfilling prophecy
   C. heritability
   D. the importance of environment on academic performance
   E. the importance of genetics on academic performance

13. A common measure of intelligence today is a test that is made up of several parts to determine an individual's intelligence score. This test is the _____.
   A. SAT
   B. AP
   C. Stanford-Binet
   D. WAIS
   E. Binet-Simon

14. The Scarr and Weinberg adoption study best illustrates what finding?
    A. Genetics is the overwhelming influence in a person's intelligence.
    B. IQ scores are strongly influenced by a person's environment.
    C. Head Start programs are ineffective.
    D. The IQ scores of identical twins are no more closely correlated than non-related children adopted into the same family.
    E. Intelligence can only be measured subjectively.

15. Which of the following can help explain racial differences in intelligence scores?
    A. Eugenics
    B. Test bias
    C. There is no racial gap.
    D. The Bell Curve
    E. A faulty formula

Sample Free Response Question

Respond to the following question using proper psychological terminology. Remember to define the selected terms and support your answer by referencing it to the situation posed.

Shayne is a ten-year-old boy with a 140 IQ. He has two brothers. Shayne is also a champion swimmer and honored banjo player. Explain each concept and discuss how each may be applied to Shayne's intelligence.
        a) giftedness
        b) Gardner's theory of multiple intelligences
        c) heritability
        d) WISC
        e) Social influences of intelligence

Sample Question Answers

Multiple Choice Questions

1. C is the correct answer. A test has validity if it measures what it sets out to measure.

2. B is the correct answer. Reliable tests yield consistent results over time.

3. D is the correct answer. Split-half reliability results in the same score on two different parts of the test.

4. C is the correct answer. Objective tests have a predetermined answer that is selected and easily scored without interpretation.

5. C is the correct answer. Inter-rater reliability is extremely important in subjective testing.

6. A is the correct answer. Remedial academic support for children was the original objective of Binet's intelligence test.

7. D is the correct answer. Early IQ scores were determined by dividing the child's mental age by his chronological age and multiplying by 100.

8. B is the correct answer. An IQ score below 70 typically classifies someone as mentally retarded.

9. C is the correct answer. A savant has a low intelligence level but an extraordinary ability in one area.

10. C is the correct answer. Spearman identified the generalized body of knowledge that underlies intelligence as the g factor.

11. B is the correct answer. Kinesthetic intelligence is bodily intelligence.

12. B is the correct answer. The self-fulfilling prophecy means that our results come from our own expectations.

13. D is the correct answer. The WAIS test is a very common instrument to measure intelligence.

14. B is the correct answer. This study showed the importance of a person's environment on intelligence scores.

15. B is the correct answer. Test biases appear to affect test scores.

Free Response Answer
This answer will be scored using a rubric. The rubric has the following points:

Terms – 5 points
Applications - 5 points

1) Giftedness is generally considered when a person has an IQ of 130 or above.
2) Shane is classified as gifted.

3) Gardener's theory of multiple intelligences supports the idea that there are seven types of intelligences.
4) Shane has kinesthetic and musical intelligence.

5) Heritability refers to the amount of variation within a group, raised under the same conditions that can be attributed to genetic differences.
6) The IQ of Shane's brother cannot be predicted from the information provided.

7) WISC is a Wechsler test that measures the level of children.
8) Shayne's IQ score was probably determined through this test.

9) Social influences on intelligence include health, education, and a nurturing environment.
10) IQ is not solely determined by environment or genetics. Shayne's intelligences are developed through social influence, including parents and siblings.

Chapter Twelve – Psychological Disorders

Psychopathology is a pattern of emotions, behavior, or thoughts that are inappropriate to a given context. They lead to distress and an inability to function in society. Other terms that are synonymous include mental disorder, mental illness and psychological disorder.

What Is Psychological Disorder?

Core Concept – The medical model takes a "disease" view, while psychology sees psychological disorder as an interaction of biological, mental, social, and behavioral factors.

Distinguishing what is normal is not an easy task. Extreme disorders can be identified easily. Severe psychopathology includes hallucinations, delusions and extreme affective disturbances. A **hallucination** is a false sensory experience. A **delusion** is a persistent false belief. A disturbance of **affect** refers to some disturbance in mood or feeling.

Identifying disorders that do not involve extreme behavior can be more difficult. There are two major conceptualizations of abnormality: the medical model and the psychological model.

Historically, it was assumed that disorders were the result of supernatural forces. Hippocrates took the first step toward a scientific study of behavior when he identified the four humors (bodily fluids) with specific temperaments. In the Middle Ages, there was a return to the use of demons and witches to explain abnormality. In the late eighteenth century, the disease model of abnormality emerged and became the **medical model.** This model held that mental disorders are diseases of the mind and can be treated as such. However, medical treatment often consisted of confinement to an asylum for the "insane."

The **psychological model** combines four perspectives: behaviorism, cognitive psychology, social learning, and biological psychology. The social perspective has become more important as psychologists acknowledge that behavior and cognition occur within a social context. The behavioral perspective says that behaviors are acquired through a system of reinforcement and environmental consequences. The cognitive perspective focuses on perceptions and thoughts. The **social-cognitive-behavioral approach** is an alternative to the medical approach. It acknowledges that abnormality is complex and arises from an interaction of these components. Bandura's psychic determinism is representative of this approach. This approach also acknowledges the role of biological factors and genetics in the development of abnormality.

While there is disagreement about the etiology or cause of mental disorders, there is agreement on the indicators. The range can be from mild to severe. The common indicators are distress, maladaptiveness, irrationality, unpredictability, and unconventionality/undesirable behavior. How many indicators are needed depends on the clinician and the disorder. It is important not to assume that one or two instances of one of these indicators means that someone has a mental disorder.

How Are Psychological Disorders Classified?

Core Concept – The DSM-IV, the most widely used system, classifies disorders by their mental and behavioral symptoms.

Disorders are classified using the Diagnostic and Statistical Manual of Mental Disorder, IV or the DSM-IV. The DSM uses five axes for diagnosis or multiaxial diagnosis. In addition to the abnormal behavior, general medical conditions as well as psychosocial functioning and environmental problems are considered. The fourth edition is quite different from previous editions. The term **neurosis,** originally meaning subjective distress, has been replaced with disorder. The term **psychosis** now means a loss of contact with reality.

Mood disorders involve a mood that is out of control. **Major depression** is the most common psychological disorder, even around the globe. The mild form is called dysthymia. Major depression is severe and involves a genetic predisposition as well as a biological basis in a decrease in certain neurotransmitters. Activity levels in the left frontal lobe are also implicated. Biology alone is not sufficient to explaining depression. A cognitive-behavioral explanation posits a negative event along with low self-esteem and a pessimistic attitude may lead to depression. Martin Seligman terms this learned helplessness. **Seasonal affective disorder** is a particular form of depression that is caused by the deprivation of sunlight.

Depression rates are higher for women. The ruminative response has been suggested as an explanation. This response is characterized by a tendency to concentrate on problems which may increase vulnerability. Seligman notes that depression is much more common today than in past times. He blames three factors: increased individualism and self-centeredness, 2) the self-esteem movement, and 3) a culture of victimology.

Another mood disorder is **bipolar disorder**. Formerly known as manic-depression, this disorder includes alternating periods of mania and profound sadness. A genetic component has been identified as contributing since the concordance rate for identical twins is about 70 percent.

Anxiety Disorders are characterized by anxiety. **Generalized Anxiety Disorder** is characterized by an ongoing sense of something wrong without an external cause. **Panic Disorder** occurs when someone experiences recurrent panic attacks with symptoms similar to those of a heart attack. There is no obvious reason for the first panic attack. Biological causes are hypothesized for panic attacks. Panic attacks can also occur with **agoraphobia** or a fear of open spaces. Severe agoraphobia may lead to becoming housebound.

Phobic disorders involve an irrational fear of a specific object or activity. Phobias are fairly common. The **preparedness hypothesis** suggests that humans are biological predisposed to learn some kinds of fears. However, these and other fears may rise to abnormally high levels. **Obsessive-compulsive disorder (OCD)** is another anxiety disorder. This disorder features unwanted thoughts that lead to compulsive behaviors. Cleaning and checking rituals are common.

Somatoform disorders involve some sort of bodily symptom or physical complaint. **Conversion disorder** is marked by the failure of some sense with no discernible physical cause. Paralysis, deafness, and blindness are common manifestations. This disorder has linkages to Freudian theory as the causes are presumed to reside in the unconscious repression of some fear. In **hypochondriasis**, people go from doctor to doctor seeking a cause and treatment for their physical aches and pains. These aches and pains often have no discernible physical cause.

Dissociative disorders involve some sort of fragmentation of the personality. **Dissociative amnesia** occurs with no physical cause and is a loss of memory for personal information. **Dissociative fugue** is similar to amnesia but the person also flees home and family and establishes a new identity and life. Fugue is extremely rare. Depersonalization disorder is a sense of having on "out-of-body" experience. This may occur after severe physical trauma. **Dissociative Identity Disorder**, formerly multiple personality disorder, has been diagnosed more in recent years. It is usually the results of severe sexual abuse in childhood and emerges as a coping mechanism. In this disorder, the individual develops distinct and separate personalities. It does not mean split personality and is generally not a psychotic break with reality.

Eating disorders are most prevalent in Western cultures. **Anorexia nervosa** is a loss of appetite and failure to eat in pursuit of thinness. If left untreated, it can lead to death. **Bulimia** is characterized by binging and purging and those with bulimia are usually normal weight.

Schizophrenia is a severe disorder in which there is a disintegration in personality and a distortion in perception. There are five major types of the disorder: disorganized, catatonic, paranoid, undifferentiated, and residual. Symptoms are divided into positive and negative. Schizophrenia is generally acknowledged as a brain disorder. It seems to require a biological predisposition that is triggered by an environmental stressor. This theory is known as the **diathesis-stress hypothesis**.

Personality disorders are a cluster of disorders in which there is maladjustment in some form. **Narcissistic personality disorder** involves an exaggerated sense of self-importance and a constant need for attention. **Antisocial personality disorder** is a long-standing pattern of irresponsible behavior and a lack of remorse of its consequences. **Borderline personality disorder** involves instability and impulsivity. The outlook for treatment of these disorders is not good. Most patients seldom seek treatment.

Other disorders are classified as **developmental disorders** since they generally first appear in childhood. **Autism** is marked by language difficulties and problems in social interaction. There is a theory-of-mind deficiency. **Dyslexia** is a reading difficulty that most likely originates in the brain. **Attention-deficit hyperactivity disorder (ADHD)** is marked by a short attention span and extreme distractibility.

What Are the Consequences of Labeling People?

Core Concept – <u>Ideally, accurate diagnoses lead to proper treatments, but diagnoses may also become labels that depersonalize individuals and ignore the social and cultural contents in which their problems arise.</u>

The debate over labeling people continues. Such labels can have long-lasting and serious impacts. It can become a cycle of neglect from the inferior status of one with a mental disorder. It can be a self-fulfilling prophecy. It can lower self-esteem. It follows the person forever. Psychologist Thomas Szasz claims that these labels are used solely to give a reason for intervention. However, a diagnostic label can allow for better treatment and more understanding.

The ecological model takes all aspects of an individual's world into account. Social and cultural contexts are considered. Even psychiatry is beginning to consider cultural issues. Three persistent myths have been identified: 1) disorders have the same prevalence in all cultures, 2) all disorder comes from biology; culture is a secondary component, and 3) culture-specific disorders appear only in exotic places.

The plea for **insanity** is a much discussed topic. Insanity is a legal, rather than a psychological, term. It refers to a person being unable to conform to a law due to a mental disorder. Several cases have shaped the laws on the insanity plea. This plea is not as successful as the public believes.

<u>Sample Multiple Choice</u>

1. Roy thinks that he is the Olympic champion in the hundred-yard dash. He is suffering from
   _____.
   A. fantasies
   B. hallucinations
   C. delusions
   D. false beliefs
   E. illusions

2. In the ancient world, psychopathology was believed to be caused by _____.
   A. demons
   B. luck
   C. illness
   D. food
   E. animals

3. Doreen laughs uncontrollably at funerals. She is exhibiting the criteria of _____.
   A. distress
   B. maladaptiveness
   C. unconventionality
   D. irrationality
   E. unpredictability

4. The major purpose of the DSM is to _____ disorders.
   A. diagnose
   B. categorize
   C. classify
   D. identify
   E. analyze

5. Lorraine's mother passed away after a long illness. Lorraine was quite sad for several months following her mother's death. When she was still in that state a year later, her friends were concerned that she might be suffering from _____.
   A. dysthymia
   B. major depression
   C. normal depression
   D. bipolar disorder
   E. anxiety disorder

6. More women than men are diagnosed with depression. One model suggests that women are more vulnerable because of their tendency towards a _____ response.
   A. thoughtful
   B. hormonal
   C. gender-linked
   D. ruminative
   E. helplessness

7. Patty went to a therapist because her behavior was causing her anxiety. Some days she was quite depressed. At other times she would go on spending sprees and stay up for three days straight. Her therapist diagnoses her with _____.
   A. panic disorder
   B. anxiety disorder
   C. bipolar disorder
   D. phobic disorder
   E. schizophrenia

8. Rupert has trouble going to social events because he cannot use the bathroom anywhere except at his own house. He is most likely suffering from _____.
    A. anxiety disorder
    B. agoraphobia
    C. obsessive-compulsive disorder
    D. major depression
    E. social phobia

9. Harvey writes for a soap opera. He has an idea for a story about a character that witnesses a murder and then loses his vision. Harvey is going to have the character develop _____.
    A. anxiety disorder
    B. obsessive-compulsive disorder
    C. major depression
    D. conversion disorder
    E. schizophrenia

10. The most common diagnosis for patients admitted to public mental health hospitals is _____.
    A. depression
    B. amnesia
    C. schizophrenia
    D. bipolar disorder
    E. paranoia

11. Neil lines his windows with aluminum foil because he fears the government is listening to his conversations. He will not talk on a public phone for the same reasons. Neil would be diagnosed with _____ schizophrenia.
    A. disorganized
    B. catatonic
    C. paranoid
    D. residual
    E. undifferentiated

12. Willard is a high level executive who has risen to the top of his profession. He did anything he had to get to his position, and he feels no remorse over doing so. He would most likely be diagnosed with _____ personality disorder.
    A. narcissistic
    B. antisocial
    C. borderline
    D. executive
    E. paranoid

13. One common element found in the histories of those diagnosed with dissociative identity disorder is a _____ .
    A. parent with mental illness
    B. viral illness as an infant
    C. genetic predisposition
    D. history of sexual abuse
    E. rich fantasy life as a child

14. Sam felt as though he was constantly in a dream or "out of his body." He would most likely be diagnosed with _____ .
    A. dissociative fugue
    B. dissociative amnesia
    C. schizophrenia
    D. bipolar disorder
    E. depersonalization disorder

15. A psychologist who believes that schizophrenia arises from the interaction of a genetic predisposition and an environmental trigger supports the _____ .
    A. double bind model
    B. diathesis-stress hypothesis
    C. interactionist view
    D. nature/nurture theory
    E. integration model

Sample Free Response Question

Respond to the following question using proper psychological terminology. Remember to define the selected terms and support your answer by referencing it to the situation posed.

Cory has difficulty leaving his house on time since it takes him so long to check everything and to make sure his bathroom is clean. He gets upset easily when his mother tries to rush him. He will yell and scream when she asks him to stop and get going.
    a) obsessive-compulsive disorder
    b) affect
    c) DSM-IV
    d) psychopathology
    e) behavioral perspective

Sample Question Answers

Multiple Choice Questions

1. C is the correct answer. A delusion is disordered thinking which is false and is the sign of a mental disorder.

2. A is the correct answer. In the ancient world, demons were assumed to be the cause of mental illness.

3. D is the correct answer. Doreen is showing irrationality, behavior that is incomprehensible to those around her. Her response is inappropriate to the situation.

4. A is the correct answer. While the DSM does classify disorders, its main purpose is to diagnose such illnesses.

5. B is the correct answer. Major depression extends beyond the ordinary timeframe for events for which some depression is normal. Lasting a year is not the norm.

6. D is the correct answer. The ruminative style of concentrating on an event is more typical of women and has been linked to the development of depression.

7. C is the correct answer. The opposite poles of manic behavior and depression would lead to a diagnosis of bipolar disorder.

8. E is the correct answer. A social phobia is characterized by an irrational fear of normal social situations.

9. D is the correct answer. In conversion disorder, a person loses function in one of the sensory organs with no physical cause.

10. A is the correct answer. Depression accounts for the majority of all admissions to mental hospitals.

11. C is the correct answer. Paranoid schizophrenia is characterized by delusions of persecution.

12. B is the correct answer. Antisocial personality disorder is characterized by a lack of regard for anyone else.

13. D is the correct answer. Most people diagnosed with Differential Identity Disorder have a history of severe sexual abuse during childhood.

14. E is the correct answer. Depersonalization disorder features a sense of being "out of body."

15. B is the correct answer. The diathesis-stress model posits an interaction between a biological predisposition and an environmental event as the cause of schizophrenia.

Free Response Answer
This question will be scored using a rubric. The rubric has the following points:

Terms- 5 points
Applications – 5 points

1) Obsessive-compulsive disorder is an anxiety disorder where obsessions turn into compulsive behavior.
2) Cory's cleaning and checking are typical of someone with OCD.

3) Affect refers to emotion or mood. It is often inappropriate in those with psychological disorders.
4) Cory's affect is inappropriate and out of proportion.

5) The DSM-IV is used to diagnose psychological disorders.
6) Cory's psychologist would use the DSM to diagnose his OCD.

7) Psychopathology is a synonym for psychological disorder that refers to behavior and emotions that are inappropriate to the situation and lead to personal difficulties.
8) Cory's behavior meets these criteria.

9) The behavioral perspective says that abnormal behavior is the result of a reinforcement system in the environment and is therefore, learned.
10) Cory is reinforced by not feeling anxious when he completes his rituals of cleaning and checking.

Chapter Thirteen – Therapies for Psychological Disorders

What Is Therapy?

Core Concept – Therapy for psychological disorders takes a variety of forms, but all involve some relationship focused on improving a person's mental, behavioral, or social functioning.

Therapy is a general term for any treatment process in psychology and psychiatry. **Therapy** refers to a variety of psychological and biomedical techniques aimed at dealing with mental disorders or coping with problems of living. People who seek treatment are called patients or clients. Access to therapy is affected by many factors including financial resources and location.

Treatment can be both **biomedical** and/or **psychological**. Biomedical treatments focus on altering the brain with drugs, psychosurgery, or electroconvulsive therapy. Psychological therapies are based on psychological principles such as learning and unconscious processes. In addition to a trusting relationship between the therapist and the patient/client, most treatments have the common components of identifying the problem, identifying the cause of the problem or the conditions that maintain the problem, and deciding on and carrying out some form of treatment.

There are several types of mental health care professionals, each with specific credentials and qualifications. These professionals are classified as counseling psychologists, clinical psychologists, psychiatrists, psychoanalysts, psychiatric nurse practitioners, clinical or psychiatric social workers, and counselors.

Ways of thinking about and treating mental disorders have varied throughout history and vary across cultures. Ancient cultures used to beat patients, while in the Middle Ages patients were confined to an asylum. Modern therapy uses a variety of approaches. How mental disorders are treated also varies with culture. Some cultures believe that disorders are a disconnect between the person and the group while others see them as a spiritual disconnect. Healing generally takes place within the culture, rather than removing the individual.

How Do Psychologists Treat Psychological Disorders?

Core Concept – Psychologists employ two main forms of treatment: the insight therapies (focused on developing understanding of the problem) and the behavior therapies (focused on changing behavior through conditioning).

Insight therapies are psychotherapies in which the therapist helps patients or clients gain insight into their problems. These therapies are sometimes called **talk therapies**. Therapists focus on their clients communicating and verbalizing emotions and motives to understand their problems. Insight therapies include Freudian psychoanalysis, neo-Freudian psychodynamic therapies, humanistic therapies, cognitive therapies, and group therapies.

Freudian psychoanalysis is the form of psychodynamic therapy developed by Sigmund Freud that has the goal of releasing conflicts and memories from the unconscious. This is accomplished through the **analysis of transference**, a Freudian technique of analyzing and interpreting the patient's relationship with the therapist. It is based on the assumption that this relationship mirrors the unresolved conflicts in the patient's past. **Neo-Freudian psychodynamic therapies** are therapies for mental disorders that were developed by psychodynamic theorists who embraced some of Freud's ideas but disagreed with others. Neo-Freudians emphasize the client's conscious motivation and the influence of experience past childhood. Relationships are also more important than in traditional psychoanalysis.

Humanistic therapies are treatments based on the assumption that people have a tendency for positive growth and self-actualization, which may be blocked by an unhealthy environment that can include negative self-evaluation and criticism from others. **Client-centered therapy** is a humanistic approach to treatment developed by Carl Rogers, emphasizing an individual's tendency for healthy psychological growth through self-actualization. A main technique in this therapy is reflection of feeling. **Reflection of feeling** is Carl Roger's technique of paraphrasing the client's words, attempting to capture the emotional tone expressed. Empathy, genuineness, and unconditional positive regard are other important elements in this approach.

Cognitive therapy emphasizes rational thinking as opposed to subjective emotion, motivation, or repressed conflict as a key to treating mental disorders. **Group therapy** is any form of psychotherapy done with more than one client or patient at a given time. Group therapy is often practiced from a humanistic perspective. **Self-help support groups** are groups, such as Alcoholics Anonymous, that provide social support and an opportunity for sharing ideas about dealing with common problems. These groups are typically organized and run by laypersons, rather than professional therapists. Couples counseling and family therapy are forms of group therapy that look at the system, not at the individual.

Behavior therapy or **behavior modification** is any form of psychotherapy based on the principles of behavioral learning, especially operant conditioning and classical conditioning. Behavior therapies include systematic desensitization, aversion therapy, contingency management, token economies, and participant modeling. **Systematic desensitization** is a behavioral technique in which anxiety is extinguished by exposing the patient to an anxiety-provoking stimulus. **Aversion therapy** is a classical conditioning procedure in which individuals are presented with an attractive stimulus paired with an unpleasant stimulation in order to condition revulsion. **Exposure therapy** is a form of desensitization in which the patient directly confronts the anxiety-provoking stimulus.

Contingency management is an operant conditioning technique approach to changing behavior by altering the consequences, especially the rewards and punishments, of behavior. **Token economy** is an operant technique applied to groups, such as classrooms or mental hospital wards, involving the distribution of "tokens" or other indicators of reinforcement contingent on desired behaviors. The tokens can later be exchanged for privileges, food, or other reinforcers. **Participant modeling** is a social learning technique in which a therapist demonstrates and encourages a client to imitate a desired behavior.

Cognitive-behavioral therapy is a form of psychotherapy that combines the techniques of cognitive therapy with those of behavioral therapy. **Rational-emotive behavior therapy (RBET)** is Albert Ellis's brand of therapy, based on the idea that irrational thoughts and behaviors are the cause of mental disorders.

Different therapeutic techniques are effective for different disorders. Behavior therapies are used for specific phobias, bedwetting, autism, and alcoholism. Cognitive-behavioral therapy is most effective with chronic pain, anorexia, bulimia, and agoraphobia. Insight therapy is effective for couples' relationship problems. Depression is best treated with a variety of therapies. A therapist should be an **active listener**, someone who gives the speaker feedback in such forms as nodding, paraphrasing, maintaining an expression that shows interest, and asking questions for clarification.

How effective is therapy? The answer is not always clear. Eysenck claimed that two-thirds of therapy patients would improve even without therapy. A survey of the research showed that therapy was more effective than no therapy and that Eysenck had overestimated the improvement rate in his no-therapy control group. Questions still exist, in particular about which therapy is truly best for which disorder.

How Is the Biomedical Approach Used to Treat Psychological Disorders?

Core Concept – Biomedical therapies seek to treat psychological disorders by changing the brain's chemistry with drugs, its circuitry with surgery, or its patterns of activity with pulses of electricity or powerful magnetic fields.

Psychopharmacology (drug therapy) is the prescribed use of drugs to help treat symptoms of mental illness to ensure that individuals are more receptive to talk therapies. Use of drugs emerged from the medical model of treatment.

Antipsychotic drugs are medicines that diminish psychotic symptoms, usually by their effect on dopamine pathways in the brain. They have a downside. An incurable disorder of motor control, especially involving muscles of the face and head, resulting from long–term use of antipsychotic drugs is called **tardive dyskinesia**.

Antidepressant drugs are medicines that are used to treat depression, usually by their effect on the serotonin and/or norepinepherine pathways in the brain. Drugs to treat depression generally fall into two types: MAOs (monoamine oxidase inhibitors) and SSRIs (selective serotonin reuptake inhibitors). Mood stabilizers include **lithium carbonate**, a simple chemical compound that is highly effective in dampening the extreme mood swings of bipolar disorder.

Anti-anxiety drugs are a category of drugs that diminish feelings of anxiety. They include barbiturates and benzodiazepines. **Stimulants** are drugs that normally increase activity level by encouraging communication among neurons in the brain. Stimulants have been found to suppress activity levels in people with **attention deficit hyperactivity disorder (ADHD)**, a common problem in children who have difficulty controlling their behavior and focusing their attention.

Other medical therapies for psychological disorders include **psychosurgery,** the general term for surgical intervention in the brain to treat psychological disorders and **electroconvulsive therapy (ECT)** a treatment used primarily for depression and involving the application of an electric current to the head, producing a generalized seizure. ECT is sometimes called "shock treatment." **Transcranial magnetic stimulation (TMS)** is a newer treatment that involves magnetic stimulation of specific regions of the brain. TMS does not produce a seizure.

The **therapeutic community** is Maxwell Jones's term for a program of treating mental disorder by making the institutional environment supportive and humane for patients. The **community mental health movement** is an effort to **deinstitutionalize** (remove patients from mental hospitals, whenever possible) mental patients and to provide therapy from outpatient clinics. Proponents of this concept envisioned that recovering patients could live with their families, in foster homes, or in group homes. However, that vision has never been fully realized.

Sample Multiple Choice Questions

1. A psychiatrist is more likely than a psychologist to _____.
    A. see patients with minor mental health problems
    B. to use the biomedical treatment for patients with mental health problems
    C. to treat clients exclusively with talk therapy
    D. use group therapy as an effective way to have clients address their mental health problems
    E. to exclusively treat clients who reside in group homes

2. Which biomedical therapy is most commonly practiced today?
    A. Psychosurgery
    B. Electroconvulsive therapy
    C. Drug therapy
    D. Transcranial magnetic stimulation
    E. Nutritional and supplements therapy

3. Matt enters therapy to talk about some issues that have been causing him distress. The therapist has earned a PhD and uses a variety of techniques to alleviate some of Matt's distressing symptoms. Matt is most likely seeing a _____.
    A. psychiatrist
    B. clinical psychologist
    C. psychiatric social worker
    D. licensed clinical social worker
    E. clinical counselor

4. _____ therapy uses techniques found in classical conditioning to develop associations between unwanted behaviors and unpleasant experiences.
   A. Behavior
   B. Psychoanalysis
   C. Humanistic
   D. Biomedical
   E. Somatic

5. _____ therapy focuses on changing unwanted behaviors rather than focusing on discovering the underlying causes of the behaviors.
   A. Behavior modification
   B. Psychoanalytic
   C. Humanistic
   D. Cognitive
   E. Group

6. The aim of cognitive-behavioral therapy is to _____.
   A. discover unconscious motives for behavior
   B. change the way people behave
   C. change the way people think and behave
   D. change peoples negative thinking patterns
   E. disassociate negative stimuli with anxiety producing events

7. Charlie is irrationally afraid of snakes. He visits Dr. Cooper to help him deal with his situation. Dr. Cooper guides him through a series of exposure to snakes, from least fear provoking to most fear provoking. Dr. Cooper probably using the treatment known as

   _____.
   A. flooding
   B. transference
   C. aversive conditioning
   D. systematic desensitization
   E. RET

8. Matt is seeking help from Dr. Blazer. Dr. Blazer's therapy for Matt helps to bring unconscious conflicts to conscious awareness so that Matt gains insight into his thoughts and behaviors. Dr. Blazer is practicing _____ therapy.
   A. biomedical
   B. RET
   C. psychoanalytic
   D. group
   E. cognitive- behavioral

9. Ann is suffering from depression and no psychological or drug therapies are working to alleviate her symptoms. The biomedical technique of _____ may be used as a last resort to help Ann
   A. flooding
   B. systematic desensitization
   C. electroconvulsive therapy
   D. psychosurgery
   E. MAO inhibitors

10. Chris is schizophrenic and his psychiatrist has prescribed Thorazine, a drug that blocks dopamine pathways. This medicine is classified in the _____ class of pharmacological drugs.
    A. stimulant
    B. antidepressant
    C. antianxiety
    D. antipsychotic
    E. depressant

11. Eleanor is encouraged to take control of her therapy sessions. Her therapist uses the active listening approach. Eleanor is likely engaged in _____ therapy.
    A. RET
    B. psychodynamic
    C. client-centered
    D. Gestalt
    E. self-help

12. Modern antidepressants, such as Prozac, work to block the reuptake of which neurotransmitter?
    A. Dopamine
    B. Serotonin
    C. Acetylcholine
    D. Norepinephrine
    E. GABA

13. _____ therapy does NOT use the services of a trained therapist.
    A. Biomedical
    B. Cognitive-behavioral
    C. Behavioral
    D. Humanistic
    E. Self-help

14. Many people suffering from mental illness are released from treatment before they should be released, due to social limits, such as insurance issues. They often end up back in treatment later for the same problems. _____ results from this practice.
    A. Greater use of skills obtained in group therapy
    B. A mental health care concern called the "revolving door" phenomenon
    C. A more productive workforce
    D. A shortage of clients for practicing therapists
    E. A lack of therapeutic techniques that are effective for short term effectiveness

15. John is a twelve-year-old who is having trouble dealing with his family's relocation to a new city. He most likely first sees first a _____.
    A. psychiatrist
    B. counselor
    C. clinical psychologist
    D. registered nurse
    E. psychoanalyst

Sample Free Response Question

Respond to the following question using proper psychological terminology. Remember to define the selected terms and support your answer by referencing it to the situation posed

Matt is diagnosed with depression. Explain how each of the following terms is related to Matt's treatment.
        a) psychiatrist
        b) SSRI
        c) cognitive-behavioral therapy
        d) ECT
        e) talk therapy

Sample Question Answers

Multiple Choice Questions

1. B is the correct answer. A psychiatrist is a medical doctor who can prescribe medicine to patients

2. C is the correct answer. Drug therapy is the most common form of biomedical therapy.

3. B is the correct answer. A clinical psychologist has a PhD and uses a variety of techniques to help clients.

4. A is the correct answer. Behavior therapy uses conditioning techniques.

5. A is the correct answer. Behavior modification concentrates on changing an individual's behavior.

6. C is the correct answer. Cognitive-behavioral therapy focuses on both thought and behavior.

7. D is the correct answer. Systematic desensitization is effective for the treatment of phobias.

8. C is the correct answer. Psychoanalysis focuses on the unconscious.

9. C is the correct answer. Electroconvulsive therapy (ECT) is used as a biomedical therapy for depression when no other therapies have been successful.

10. D is the correct answer. Thorazine falls into the category of antipsychotic medications.

11. C is the correct answer. In client centered therapy, the therapist takes a non-directive approach.

12. B is the correct answer. SSRIs, like Prozac, block the reuptake of serotonin.

13. E is the correct answer. Self-help groups generally do not use the resources of a trained therapist.

14. B is the correct answer. There is a mental health care crisis in our country that contributes to lack of adequate treatment and support due to fiscal constraints.

15. B is the correct answer. Counselors generally deal with less severe mental problems.

Free Response Answer
This answer will be scored using a rubric. The rubric has the following points.

Terms – 5 points
Applications – 5 points

1) Psychiatrists are medical doctors (MD) who can prescribe medication for depression.
2) Depression has a biochemical component that would need a psychiatrist's care if medication is needed for treatment.

3) SSRIs (selective serotonin reuptake inhibitor) are a class of drugs used to alter the balance of serotonin the brain.
4) Prozac is an SSRI that may be prescribed because a chemical imbalance of serotonin is associated with depression.

5) Cognitive-behavioral therapy is a form of psychotherapy that combines the techniques of cognitive therapy with those of behavioral therapy.
6) The therapist would try to get Matt to change his thought processes and behaviors.

7) ECT electroconvulsive therapy is a treatment used primarily for depression and involving the application of an electric current to the head, producing a generalized seizure.
8) ECT is a last resort for the treatment of depression. It would be used if nothing else works.

9) Talk therapies are psychotherapies that focus on communicating and verbalizing emotions and motives to understand their problems.
10) Matt would be advised to obtain talk therapy in conjunction with his biomedical therapy.

Chapter 14 – Social Psychology

Social psychology is the branch of psychology that looks at the impact of social variables and how behavior, thoughts and feelings are influenced by interaction with others. The **social context** is the combination of people, activities, interactions, the settings, the expectations, and social norms that govern behavior. It is not the objective reality that is important but our subjective reality.

How Does the Social Situation Affect Our Behavior?

Core Concept – We usually adapt our behavior to the demands of the social situation and in ambiguous situations we take our cues from the behavior of others in that setting.

Situationism assumes that the behavioral context can have powerful effects on behavior. It contrasts with dispositionism which assumes that behavior is the result of internal factors.

The response in most situations depends upon a person's social roles and the group's social norms. **Social roles** are socially defined patterns of behavior that are expected in specific situations. People play many social roles. At times, we use **scripts** which are clusters of knowledge about events and actions expected in a particular situation. The students in the Stanford Prison Experiment used such scripts to guide their behavior at the beginning of the experiment.

Groups also develop unwritten rules about how members of the group should behave. These expectations are called **social norms** and they tell people what socially appropriate attitudes and behaviors are. These norms can be broad guidelines or specific standards. They govern all aspects of behavior, including dress, conversation and conduct. Theodore Newcomb's study at Bennington College showed how such norms can even influence political views.

How powerful are the social pressures? The tendency to imitate others is called the chameleon effect. Can the situation really influence behavior? Solomon Asch demonstrated that it can in his study of conformity. **Conformity** is the tendency for people to adopt the behaviors and attitudes of others in a group. In Asch's study he found that participants conformed to blatantly incorrect behavior three-quarters of the time. His results have been replicated many times and have come to be known as the **Asch effect**.

Not everyone will conform, though, especially in situations such as that in the Asch study. Heroes are individuals who are able to resist this peer pressure in the face of what is called the challenge of individual heroic defiance.

Asch identified three factors that influence whether or not someone will give in to group pressure. They are the size of the majority, the presence of a partner who dissents from the majority and the size of the discrepancy. Other researchers have identified additional factors including a difficult or ambiguous judgment task, a perception of competent group members, public responses, and unanimity of the majority.

Groups may also face pressure to conform. This process of group conformity is called groupthink and happens when individuals go along with what they perceive to be the group consensus. Six conditions make groupthink more likely. The conditions are 1) isolation of group, 2) high cohesiveness, 3) directive leadership, 4) lack of norms about processes, 5) member homogeneity, and 6) high external stress.

Individuals can also command authority and obedience. Stanley Milgram conducted the most famous experiment on obedience. His methodology is controversial given today's ethical standards. His results demonstrated that most people would obey even if they thought they were causing harm to someone. Several conditions have been identified as conditions that foster obedience. They are 1) when a peer models obedience, 2) when the victim is remote, 3) when the authority figure is directly watching, 4) when a participant acts as an intermediary bystander, and 5) when the authority figure has higher status.

Study of the bystander issue began with the Kitty Genovese incident in which no one assisted a woman who was being attacked. Latane and Darley devised a series of studies to examine why. Response to a problem depended on the number of bystanders present. When there was a large group, **diffusion of responsibility** occurred. Two studies suggest that the bystander problem can be mediated by appropriate training. The researcher also found that the best way to get help is to ask for it and to reduce the ambiguity of the situation by clearly explaining the problem.

Constructing Social Reality: What Influences Our Judgments of Others?

Core Concepts – The judgments we make about others depend not only on their behavior but also on our interpretations of their actions within a social context.

Our **social reality** is our subjective interpretations of other people and of our relationships. It influences many areas of life.

Relationships are important to most people. The **reward theory of attraction** says we like best those who give us maximum rewards at minimum costs. There are four powerful sources of rewards that predict interpersonal attraction. The sources are proximity, similarity, self-disclosure, and physical attractiveness. The **principle of proximity** says we will make friends with those who are physically close by, such as at work or in the neighborhood. The **similarity principle** says we are attracted to those who are most similar to ourselves. Attraction is enhanced when we share personal details and when people are attractive. There are exceptions to this theory since many relationships do not seem to be particularly rewarding.

The notion that we end up with mates at about our same level of attractiveness is known as the **matching hypothesis. Expectancy-value theory** says that we decide to pursue a relationship by weighing the potential value of the relationship against the expectation of success in the relationship. **Cognitive dissonance** explains why people may stay in relationships that do not work. This theory says that we are only motivated to change when the cognitive conflicts become overwhelming.

Cognitive attributions are the cognitive explanations we make for behavior, ours and others. Most of us commit the **fundamental attribution error**. The FAE is the tendency to emphasize in others the internal reasons for behaviors (dispositions) and diminish the external reasons (situations). The **self-serving bias** is a pattern in which we take credit for our successes but not for our failures.

Prejudice is a particular type of attitude. It is a negative attitude about an individual based solely on that individual's group membership. **Discrimination** is a negative action against an individual based on group membership. The principles of **in-group** and **out-group** and **social distance** contribute to prejudice. Economic competition is another contributor. A third cause of prejudice is **scapegoating** which is blaming someone else for one's own problems. Other causes include conformity to social norms and media stereotypes.

Ways of combating prejudice include creating new role models, creating situations where there is equal status contact, and legislation.

Social psychology covers many other topics. **Social facilitation** is when an individual's performance improves due to being in a group. **Social loafing** is a decrease in performance due to being in a group. **Deindividuation** occurs when an individual loses a sense of self due to group membership. **Group polarization** is when there are differences of opinion in a group and those opinions become extreme. **Groupthink** occurs when group members look for consensus without really considering the issues.

Love is another topic studied in social psychology. **Romantic love** has been defined as a condition including infatuation and sexual interest. Robert Sternberg developed a **triangular theory of love**. He posits three types of love: romantic, infatuation, and consummate or complete love.

What Are the Roots of Violence and Terrorism?

Core Concept – The power of the situation can help us understand violence and terrorism but a broader understanding requires multiple perspectives that go beyond the boundaries of traditional psychology.

Violence and **aggression** are behaviors that are intended to harm others. An early study of these tendencies was the Robbers' Cave study by Muzafer Sherif. **Cohesiveness,** or a sense of group membership, and **mutual interdependence**, a shared sense that others are needed to accomplish a goal, emerged as important elements in eliminating group conflict.

Terrorism has been fueled by poverty, powerlessness, and hopelessness. **Terrorism** is the use of violent and unpredictable acts by a small group against a larger group. It is based on political, economic, or religious goals. Herbert Kelman has developed an approach for conflict resolution based on the Robbers' Cave study.

Sample Multiple Choice Questions

1. Darla believes that it is a person's innate qualities that determine how they behave. This idea reflects the concept of _____.
   A. interactionism
   B. situationism
   C. dispositionism
   D. innatism
   E. behaviorism

2. At work you are an employee. That is an example of a social _____.
   A. role
   B. function
   C. character
   D. job
   E. position

3. Sarah likes to dress like Britney Spears. She sings Britney's music and changes her hair as Britney changes hers. This tendency to mimic is called the _____ effect.
   A. imitation
   B. replication
   C. chameleon
   D. simulation
   E. impersonation

4. The Asch study demonstrated what has come to be known as the Asch Effect. In his study, Asch examined the impact of _____.
   A. a group majority on the judgments of an individual
   B. an individual's opinion on a unanimous group decision
   C. a researcher's presence upon group decisions
   D. the influence of friends on group opinions
   E. a group's size upon the judgment of an individual

5. Based on Milgram's experiment, we concluded that people are most likely to be obedient under all of the following conditions except when _____.
   A. a peer models obedience
   B. the victim was remote from the subject
   C. the authority figure had higher relative status
   D. the teacher was under direct surveillance
   E. the authority figure was wearing a lab coat

6. The best predictor of bystander intervention is _____.
   A. ethnicity of the bystanders
   B. ethnicity of the victim
   C. the number of bystanders
   D. the location of the emergency
   E. the time of day of the emergency

7. We tend to like people who like us, with whom we exchange gifts, and with whom we can share interests. This demonstrates what is called the _____ theory of attraction.
   A. exchange
   B. similarity
   C. complementary
   D. reward
   E. compensation

8. Pippa and Buster have been dating for two years. They were both voted best looking in their senior class. Their relationship demonstrates the _____ hypothesis.
   A. similarity
   B. prettiness
   C. attractiveness
   D. charisma
   E. matching

9. Julie thought all football players were fairly dumb. Then she met the quarterback Bert a magna cum laude graduate with a Rhodes scholarship. Julie experienced _____.
   A. cognitive dissonance
   B. cognitive disbelief
   C. incredulity
   D. skepticism
   E. cognitive mistrust

10. Sally tripped on the rug when she entered the dorm. She blamed it on the rug being slippery. When Stuart did the same thing, she called him clumsy. This is representative of _____.
    A. the self-serving bias
    B. cognitive dissonance
    C. the fundamental attribution error
    D. attribution dissonance
    E. an ascription error

11. Gerry got an A in psychology but a C in calculus. He explained his psychology grade by his hard work and his calculus grade by the teacher's tests. He is exhibiting _____.
    A. the self-serving bias
    B. cognitive dissonance
    C. the fundamental attribution error
    D. attribution dissonance
    E. an ascription error

12. A strategy for reducing conflict based on the Robbers' Cave experiment involves _____.
    A. meeting aggression with aggression
    B. scapegoating the perpetrators of terrorism
    C. winning competitions by a large margin
    D. finding common goals with our enemies
    E. ignoring acts of aggression against us

13. Stacy has never met anyone from Bora Bora. She tells her classmates that such people must be savages and not know much. She is exhibiting _____.
    A. discrimination
    B. bias
    C. prejudice
    D. bigotry
    E. intolerance

14. You understand that as a student, you come into class, sit down, take out your books, paper, and pen and get ready to take notes. You listen to the teacher and ask questions. That is your _____ as a student.
    A. role
    B. schema
    C. function
    D. responsibility
    E. script

15. Which of the following is true about social distance?
    A. Reducing social distance and prejudice cannot be mandated by law.
    B. The in-group members serve to decrease social distance towards newcomers.
    C. Social distance can only be reduced through scapegoating.
    D. As social distance increases, so does the potential for prejudice.
    E. Social distance is necessary for groups to coexist.

Sample Free Response Question

Respond to the following question using proper psychological terminology. Remember to define the selected terms and support your answer by referencing the situation posed.

Jacquie and Lisa are part of a group at the local high school that is trying to end the cliquishness in the high school that has led to fights after school. Explain how what each of the following terms means and how it might contribute to the situation.

        a) prejudice
        b) in-group
        c) social norms
        d) scapegoating
        e) equal status contact

Sample Question Answers

Multiple Choice Questions

1. C is the correct answer. Dispositionism is the belief that behavior is the result of internal factors such as genes, traits, and character.

2. A is the correct answer. A social role consists of expected patterns of behavior within a given setting.

3. C is the correct answer. The chameleon effect is the term for the tendency to mimic others.

4. A is the correct answer. Asch examined the influence of the group majority on individual's opinions.

5. E is the correct answer. All of the other conditions lead to obedience.

6. C is the correct answer. The best predictor of intervention is the number of people around the emergency.

7. D is the correct answer. The reward theory of attraction states we look for people whom we like and with whom we share interests, thus gaining reward.

8. E is the correct answer. The matching hypothesis says that we find friends and mates who are perceived to be the same level of attractiveness.

9. A is the correct answer. Cognitive dissonance occurs when there is a conflict between beliefs and actions.

10. C is the correct answer. When we attribute behavior of others to internal characteristics rather than the situation we are committing the fundamental attribution error.

11. A is the correct answer. With the self-serving bias we attribute our successes to internal factors and our failure to external factors.

12. D is the correct answer. The Robbers' Cave study showed that working toward a common goal reduced conflict between groups.

13. C is the correct answer. Prejudice is a negative attitude toward a person based solely on their group membership.

14. E is the correct answer. A script is a cluster of knowledge of behaviors expected in a specific situation.

15. D is the correct answer. When groups perceive social distance, they tend not to see others as equal and this prejudice increases.

Free Response Answer
This question would be scored using a rubric. The rubric has the following points:

Terms – 5 points
Application – 5 points

1) Prejudice is a negative attitude about a person based solely on group membership.
2) Members of each group are prejudiced towards the other group.

3) In-group is the group with which each person identifies.
4) Each group thinks of themselves as the in-group.

5) Social norms are the unwritten rules governing group behavior.
6) Each group has its own social norms which may include fighting.

7) Scapegoating occurs when one group blames the other for its own problems.
8) One group at the school blamed the other for losing an important football game.

9) Equal status contact occurs when groups are placed together and neither has power over the other.
10) The girls can use this concept in their work on reducing the tension.

Sample AP Exam

Sample Multiple Choice Questions

You have seventy minutes to answer these questions. Remember that there is a correction in scoring, so only guess if you can eliminate one or more of the options.

1. Psychology is the scientific study of _____.
    A. human and animal behavior
    B. behavior and mental disturbance
    C. behavior and mental processes
    D. human behavior and animal instincts
    E. mental disorders and treatment

2. The perspective of _____ psychology is most closely associated with the study of attending, thinking, knowing, and remembering.
    A. behaviorist
    B. cognitive
    C. psychoanalytic
    D. biological
    E. humanistic

3. The perspective of _____ psychology assumes that humans behave because of unconscious conflicts.
    A. behaviorist
    B. cognitive
    C. psychoanalytic
    D. humanistic
    E. biological

4. Gera works for the local newspaper. He is writing an article about SAT scores in the different high schools in the district. He divides the students into groups based on gender and school attended. He then examines SAT scores. In this study, the independent variable is the _____.
    A. school the students attend
    B. college of choice
    C. income level of the parents
    D. gender of the students
    E. SAT scores of the students

5. Gera works for the local newspaper. He is writing an article about SAT scores in the different high schools in the district. He divides the students into groups based on gender and school attended. He then examines SAT scores. In this study, the dependent variable is the _____.
    A. school the students attend
    B. college of choice
    C. income level of the parents
    D. gender of the students
    E. SAT scores of the students

6. Professor Ripken is interested in studying children's social behaviors. To do this, he visits a preschool and carefully monitors and records the children's behavior. Professor Ripken is engaged in _____ research.
    A. survey
    B. naturalistic observation
    C. case study
    D. longitudinal
    E. experimental

7. Gera looked at the statistical relationship between SAT scores and high school grades. He found that as SAT scores went up, so did high school grades. This is an examples of a(n) _____ correlation.
    A. learned
    B. positive
    C. zero
    D. negative
    E. academic

8. Alicia wants to understand peer pressure among adolescents so she goes to a popular mall and ask teenagers to complete a questionnaire about their friends. Alicia is using _____.
    A. survey research
    B. a case study
    C. introspection
    D. cross-sectional research
    E. naturalistic observation

9. Rupert wants to learn whether men or women are better drivers. To determine this, he decides that he will measure driving ability by examining the number of tickets that people have been received. He is using the number of tickets as the basis of his _____.
    A. control group
    B. theory of good driving
    C. independent variable
    D. operational definition
    E. hypothesis

10. The supposition that a researcher makes about the variables in the study being conducted is called a(n) _____.
    A. hypothesis
    B. theory
    C. guess
    D. variable
    E. correlation

11. Delia was in a car accident in which she hit her head. Now she can no longer remember any new information. She most likely damaged her _____.
    A. occipital lobes
    B. cerebral cortex
    C. reticular activating system
    D. hippocampus
    E. thalamus

12. Allison was in a car accident and injured her head. Now she has a great deal of trouble seeing things clearly. She most likely injured the _____ lobe of her brain.
    A. occipital
    B. frontal
    C. cerebral
    D. parietal
    E. temporal

13. Which is an example of a parasympathetic response?
    A. Getting ready to take an exam
    B. Running on a treadmill
    C. Breathing slowly to get to sleep
    D. Watching the Super Bowl
    E. Watching a horror movie

14. The peripheral nervous system is comprised of which two subdivisions?
    A. The parasympathetic nervous system and the autonomic nervous system
    B. The autonomic nervous system and the sympathetic nervous system
    C. The autonomic nervous system and the central nervous system
    D. The somatic nervous system and the autonomic nervous system
    E. The somatic nervous system and the sympathetic nervous system

15. The part of the brain MOST associated with emotions is the _____.
    A. medulla
    B. reticular activating system
    C. thalamus
    D. hypothalamus
    E. amygdala

16. Your grandmother has trouble breathing and she is having trouble regulating her blood pressure. The part of her brain that is no longer working as it should is the _____.
    A. hippocampus
    B. pons
    C. medulla
    D. amygdala
    E. thalamus

17. Stan is having trouble remembering. His neurologist is trying to figure out what is going on in Stan's brain. The neurologist uses the _____ test to see which brains cells are most active while Stan does calculus.
    A. MRI
    B. fMRI
    C. EEG
    D. CAT scan
    E. PET scan

18. If you go to a horror movie and get goose bumps, you can thank your _____ nervous system.
    A. autonomic
    B. somatic
    C. peripheral
    D. sympathetic
    E. parasympathetic

19. When you are able to correctly identify that the noise you hear after going to bed as just your cat jumping on the dining room table, your ability to accurately identify that noise is due to _____.
    A. your good hearing
    B. your past experience
    C. a perceptual set
    D. sensation principles
    E. signal detection theory

20. Negative afterimages are explained by the _____ theory of color vision.
    A. rod and cone
    B. afterimage
    C. opponent-process
    D. color blindness
    E. trichromatic

21. You take acetaminophen to lessen the pain of your headache. The idea that such drugs can stop the pain comes from the _____ theory of pain.
    A. drug-control
    B. gate-control
    C. placebo
    D. neural firing
    E. sensory pathway

22. Infants develop depth perception at the age of _____ months.
    A. three
    B. eighteen
    C. nine
    D. six
    E. twelve

23. Jeff swims on his school's team. He has a false start in his race and is disqualified. He dove off the blocks early due to his anticipation of the gun firing. This is due to _____.
    A. experience
    B. anticipation
    C. context
    D. practice
    E. perceptual set

24. Sharon had trouble hearing the teacher so the school gave her a hearing test. Some of the sounds presented were at such a low level of intensity that she could hardly hear them. These sounds were below her _____ threshold.
    A. absolute
    B. difference
    C. discriminative
    D. adaptive
    E. sensory

25. Sandy is having her eyes tested in the optician's office. One of the eye charts looks like this:
    XX XX
    XX XX
    XX XX
    XX XX

    She sees it as two columns of Xs, rather than four rows. At work here is the Gestalt principle of _____.
    A. Pragnanz
    B. closure
    C. proximity
    D. continuity
    E. common fate

26. The deepest point in the sleep cycle occurs in _____ sleep.
    A. Stage 1
    B. Stage 2
    C. Stage 3
    D. REM
    E. Stage 4

27. Joey gets up at 2:00 a.m. and begins to sleepwalk around the dorm halls. An EEG of his brain waves would most likely indicate _____ waves.
    A. delta
    B. sigma
    C. theta
    D. beta
    E. alpha

28. Psychologists and other researchers believe that hypnosis is not appropriate for _____.
    A. relaxation
    B. pain control
    C. memory enhancement
    D. phobia control
    E. reducing anxieties

29. Your English teacher likes to give unannounced quizzes. He is using a _____ schedule of reinforcement.
    A. variable ratio
    B. continuous
    C. fixed ratio
    D. variable interval
    E. fixed interval

30. When you push the buttons on the vending machine and get your soda, the process of _____ is at work.
    A. classical conditioning
    B. operant conditioning
    C. habituation
    D. cognitive learning
    E. punishment

31. You were conditioned to smile when you hear the ice cream truck bell. During the winter, this response diminishes. However, in June when you hear a bell that sounds similar, you begin to smile again. In classical conditioning, the return of this response is known as _____.
    A. extinction
    B. reconditioning
    C. discrimination
    D. spontaneous recovery
    E. generalization

32. The child for whom you baby-sit throws tantrums in order to get his way every time you are with him. When you give in to his demands to make the tantrum stop, you have been _____.
    A. negatively punished
    B. positively reinforced
    C. negatively reinforced
    D. positively punished
    E. classically conditioned

33. The lights at school went out and it was pitch dark in the room. You were able to navigate to the room because of a(n)_____ map.
    A. recall
    B. cognitive
    C. ecological
    D. memory
    E. environmental

34. Your sister loses a DVD that belongs to your dad and really gets into any trouble. The next weekend, you are tempted to borrow one but remember what happened to your sister and leave the DVDs alone. This type of learning is best explained by _____.
    A. social learning
    B. classical conditioning
    C. operant conditioning
    D. trial and error
    E. insight learning

35. The biological process most implicated in learning involves _____.
    A. efferent neurons
    B. synapses
    C. hormones
    D. the hippocampus
    E. serotonin

36. Jane went to the show at Sea World where it was over a hundred degrees. She fainted. Now if she sees a dolphin she feels queasy. The dolphin has become a(n) _____.
    A. unconditioned stimulus
    B. unconditioned response
    C. neutral stimulus
    D. conditioned stimulus
    E. conditioned response

37. Your friend can look at a complex figure and remember every detail. The memory involved in this type of task is _____ memory.
    A. picture
    B. pattern
    C. iconic
    D. eidetic
    E. visual

38. You have studied the terms you need to pass this test. When you read the terms, you hold them in _____ memory in order to process them
    A. sensory
    B. recall
    C. long-term
    D. working
    E. retrieval

39. You have been studying all night for your psychology test. You are having trouble remembering how to spell Erik Erikson's name, so you keep repeating it over and over as you walk to your classroom to take the test. This is an example of _____.
    A. studying correctly
    B. maintenance rehearsal
    C. elaborative rehearsal
    D. working rehearsal
    E. relational studying

40. You are at the airport waiting to check in for your flight home. You see a man who looks very familiar. You cannot remember his name. Later when you get airborne, you remember that he is on one of your favorite television shows. Your inability to remember his name highlights _____.
    A. hippocampal failure
    B. anterograde amnesia
    C. encoding-specificity
    D. retrograde amnesia
    E. retrieval failure

41. When you hear the term *flower*, you think of a rose. Rose is your _____ of a flower.
    A. concept
    B. heuristic
    C. scheme
    D. prototype
    E. mental representation

42. Your psychology professor has assigned a research paper. It is due at the end of the term. She requires you to turn in several preliminary steps. She is teaching you to use a problem solving strategy called _____.
    A. searching for analogies
    B. trial and error
    C. working backward
    D. creating subgoals
    E. preliminary work

43. Mary completed Algebra I last year. Now, in Algebra II, she tries to solve the problems in the same way as she did last year. She cannot seem to use new strategies. Mary is demonstrating _____.
    A. functional fixedness
    B. prototypical modeling
    C. availability bias
    D. mental set
    E. perceptual set

44. Addie was analyzing the baseball game that her team lost on Monday morning. She maintained that the manager should have changed pitchers in the third inning although she made no such comment during the game. This is an example of the _____ bias.
    A. availability
    B. anchoring
    C. representativeness
    D. confirmation
    E. hindsight

45. When all intelligence test scores fall under a bell-shaped curve, we call that a(n) _____.
    A. intelligence curve
    B. random distribution
    C. normal distribution
    D. random curve
    E. intelligence distribution

46. Melissa has been studying intelligence in her psychology class. One concept she finds interesting in heritability. She explains to her mother that the term means _____.
   A. that almost all of intelligence is inherited
   B. the amount of trait similarity within a group attributed to genetics
   C. the amount of trait variation within a group attributed to genetics
   D. that very little of intelligence is inherited
   E. some intelligence may be inherited but some may not be inherited

47. "We feel sorry because we cry" represents the _____ theory of emotion.
   A. James-Lange
   B. Cannon- Bard
   C. LeDoux
   D. Ekman
   E. Schachter

48. You were outside playing basketball in the hot sun for three hours. You got really thirsty and rushed inside where you drank a whole quart of Gatorade. Your behavior can best be explained by _____ theory.
   A. instinct
   B. drive reduction
   C. arousal
   D. cognitive
   E. locus of control

49. You scored poorly on your math final because you never did any of the homework problems, nor did you study for any of the tests. You blame your failure on yourself because you did not study as you should have. You are exhibiting a(n) _____ locus of control.
   A. intrinsic
   B. extrinsic
   C. cognitive
   D. internal
   E. external

50. Melanie opened her purse to grab her cell phone to make an important call about a job interview. She rummaged through her purse but could not find the phone, and her heart began to beat quickly. She was experiencing _____.
   A. a hassle
   B. panic
   C. burnout
   D. chronic stress
   E. acute stress

51. When Melanie felt stress, the part of her brain that responded first was the _____.
    A. hippocampus
    B. thalamus
    C. cerebral cortex
    D. hypothalamus
    E. amygdala

52. Marian felt her heart start to race and her palms got sweaty as the AP Psychology exam began. According to Selye's General Adaptation Syndrome, she is in the stage of _____.
    A. fear
    B. resistance
    C. inhibition
    D. alarm
    E. withdrawal

53. You are hiking in the mountains when you unexpectedly encounter a wild dog who bares his teeth at you. Immediately your _____ system kicks into gear.
    A. autonomic nervous
    B. peripheral nervous
    C. emotion focused
    D. parasympathetic nervous
    E. somatic nervous

54. Biologically speaking, the goal of sex is to _____.
    A. have many offspring
    B. find a mate
    C. achieve release
    D. release sex hormones
    E. enjoy the feelings

55. Movement in the fetus is generally detected first in the _____ week.
    A. fourth
    B. sixteenth
    C. eleventh
    D. eighth
    E. twentieth

56. According to the work of Ainsworth, children who experience attachment problems _____.
    A. will definitely experience attachment problems as adults
    B. are likely to experience mental problems
    C. will most probably experience emotional extremes
    D. are likely to become workaholics and avoid people
    E. can succeed in overcoming attachment problems

57. The understanding that superficial physical properties of an object do not affect its essence is called _____.
   A. conservation
   B. intransience
   C. centration
   D. animistic thought
   E. object permanence

58. Our innate disposition is called our _____.
   A. attachment style
   B. personality
   C. character
   D. temperament.
   E. nature

59. Robin's mother encourages her to try her best and to work toward her own goals. When she sets rules, she explains why to Robin. This is an example of the _____ parenting style.
   A. authoritarian
   B. authoritative
   C. permissive
   D. neglectful
   E. uninvolved

60. According to Piagetian theory, adolescents in the formal operational stage would be better suited for which of the following tasks than would someone in the concrete operational stage?
   A. Designing an experiment to measure the effects of study skills on grades
   B. Learning to speak a second language
   C. Identifying the important battles in the Civil War
   D. Memorizing the capitals of the fifty states
   E. Solving a series of multiplication problems

61. Samantha says she doesn't hit her younger brother, Justin, because if she did hit him, her mother would punish her. According to Kohlberg's theory, this demonstrates stage _____ of Kohlberg's moral development?
   A. 1
   B. 2
   C. 3
   D. 4
   E. 5

62. Erikson views _____ as the primary challenge facing older adults.
    A. generativity versus stagnation
    B. ego integrity versus despair
    C. identity versus role confusion
    D. intimacy versus isolation
    E. initiative versus guilt

63. Which of the following statements most accurately summarizes the current view of most psychologists regarding the issue of nature and nurture?
    A. Genes determine everything in life.
    B. Genes have little influence on our development.
    C. It depends on what area of development.
    D. Environment and genes interact.
    E. It's not really a discussion.

64. All of Freud's ego defense mechanisms operate at the _____ level.
    A. conscious
    B. preconscious
    C. subconscious
    D. unconscious
    E. postconscious

65. Mary does not earn very good grades on her final paper. She decides to cheat on her final exam so that she can pass her class. She says "everyone is doing it so cheating is okay." Mary is using the defense mechanism of _____.
    A. denial
    B. repression
    C. reaction formation
    D. rationalization
    E. sublimation

66. Sally watched her older sister get out of doing her chores by whining to their parents. When it was time for Sally to do her chores, she whined about the work to her mother. Sally's behavior is reflective of the theory of _____.
    A. Freud
    B. Horney
    C. Bandura
    D. Rotter
    E. Maslow

67.	Angela works hard to earn high marks on her papers and exams. Rotter would say that Angela has a _____ locus of control.
A.	cognitive
B.	internal
C.	external
D.	positive
E.	intrinsic

68.	One of the criticisms of the social-cognitive theories is that they _____.
A.	are not based on research
B.	do not include therapeutic techniques
C.	are not as comprehensive as other theories
D.	emphasize rational information processing
E.	are not testable

69 .	An exemplary personality test or inventory must have _____.
A.	clarity
B.	simplicity
C.	a theory base
D.	reliability
E.	precision

70.	Jack seems to be very conscientious at work but he often is lackadaisical at home and fails to complete his chores. Whose theory would best explain his personality?
A.	Freud
B.	Maslow
C.	Mischel
D.	Jung
E.	Rotter

71.	The purpose of the Binet and Simon's first test was to _____.
A.	identify students who were gifted
B.	measure IQ of French students
C.	collect statistics for research
D.	decide who went on to high school
E.	identify students who need remediation

72.	Your brother does better on tests that measure the ability to see relationships and solve problems. Cattell would say he is strong in _____ intelligence.
A.	general
B.	analytical
C.	crystallized
D.	specialized
E.	fluid

73. Fritz is eight years old. He scores at ten years as his mental age. What is his IQ according to the traditional formula?
    A. 125
    B. 160
    C. 80
    D. 100
    E. 119

74. Which theorist would argue that elite-level athletes and ballet dancers have a specific intelligence involving bodily-kinesthetic abilities?
    A. Sternberg
    B. Wechsler
    C. Guilford
    D. Gardner
    E. Cattell

75. Social class affects intelligence in terms of all of the following except _____.
    A. nutrition
    B. housing
    C. parenting
    D. health care
    E. education

76. Evidence suggests that the direct biological triggering mechanism for panic disorder lies in the _____.
    A. genes
    B. brain stem
    C. limbic system
    D. endocrine system
    E. hypothalamus

77. A study by the National Institute of Mental Health found that _____ percent of the population suffers from psychological disorders.
    A. 30
    B. 25
    C. 5
    D. 10
    E. 15

78. Janet's therapist believes that her phobia came about from her mother who rewarded her fear of public speaking by soothing her with ice cream and candy. Her therapist most likely is a proponent of the _____ perspective.
   A. cognitive
   B. humanistic
   C. social
   D. behavioral
   E. psychodynamic

79. Your friend Sam was so overwhelmed with anxiety that he could not bring himself to take the Graduate Record Exam. He is displaying the indicator of abnormality called

   _____.
   A. distress
   B. maladaptiveness
   C. irrationality
   D. unpredictability
   E. unconventionality

80. Which DSM-IV category covers disorders in which an individual is overly concerned with issues of physical health?
   A. Dissociative disorders
   B. Affective disorders
   C. Somatoform disorders
   D. Organic disorders
   E. Personality disorders

81. A particular form of depression related to sunlight deprivation is known as _____.
   A. clinical depression
   B. seasonal affective disorder
   C. sunlight deprivation disorder
   D. winter latitude disorder
   E. darkness depression

82. Research on the cause of schizophrenia has lately focused on the neurotransmitter

   _____.
   A. serotonin
   B. acetycholine
   C. dopamine
   D. glutamate
   E. GABA

83. Children with autism exhibit all of the following symptoms **except** _____.
    A. a theory of mind
    B. social isolation
    C. language difficulties
    D. hyperactivity
    E. repetitive behavior

84. Marilyn Monroe was known for quickly changing moods and difficult relationships. She had little tolerance for frustration. A psychologist would most likely diagnose her with _____ personality disorder.
    A. borderline
    B. paranoid
    C. antisocial
    D. narcissistic
    E. histrionic

85. Simon has a private practice and works with clients who have problems related to mood disorders. To help them, he prescribes antidepressant drugs. Simon is most likely a _____.
    A. psychologist
    B. social worker
    C. pastoral counselor
    D. psychiatrist
    E. pharmacist

86. A shared assumption of the insight therapies is that the distressed person needs to _____.
    A. develop an understanding of the underlying difficulties
    B. be given medication to help them cope with the difficulty
    C. spend years in therapy working on the difficulty
    D. delve into the relationship with both parents
    E. change the family system in which they live

87. Rational-Emotive Therapy attempts to challenge the _____.
    A. "shoulds" and "oughts"
    B. client environment
    C. client's reward system
    D. "musts" and "supposed tos"
    E. client's memories of childhood

88. Ben is working with a client. His major technique involves reflective listening. Ben is following the therapy approach of _____.
   A. Sigmund Freud
   B. Carl Rogers
   C. Aaron Beck
   D. Karen Horney
   E. Abraham Maslow

89. The community mental health movement focuses on _____.
   A. treatment
   B. drug therapy
   C. de-institutionalizion
   D. home situations
   E. prevention

90. Caitlyn is a behavioral therapist. She has a client who is deathly afraid of garden snakes. Caitlyn has her client watch a video of snakes. This is a process known as _____.
   A. aversion therapy
   B. reflective watching
   C. symbolic modeling
   D. free association
   E. systematic desensitization

91. Anti-depressant drugs work through a process known as _____.
   A. inhibition
   B. reuptake
   C. transmission
   D. resistance
   E. absorption

92. The neo-Freudian perspective on treating psychological disorder differs from traditional Freudian therapy in the emphasis on _____.
   A. information-processing problems
   B. neurotransmitter and hormone imbalances
   C. deficient social support
   D. genetic predispositions
   E. nutrition and exercise

93. The participants in the Stanford Prison Experiment learned _____.
   A. never to volunteer for research
   B. how to conduct a research study
   C. what can happen in a real prison
   D. the situation strongly influences behavior
   E. innate personality qualities determine behavior

94. A key element that needs to be present in order to label a behavior as aggressive is
    _____.
    A. physical harm
    B. violence
    C. intent
    D. hostility
    E. cruelty

95. The unwritten rules for group behavior are called social _____.
    A. rules
    B. scripts
    C. customs
    D. models
    E. norms

96. If you are in trouble, you are most likely to get help from others if _____.
    A. there is more than one person around
    B. you are seriously injured
    C. ask for help
    D. you offer a reward for helping
    E. there is a camera nearby

97. Conformity is the tendency to _____.
    A. adopt the behavior and attitudes of others
    B. be influenced by private expectations of how others will act
    C. behave in ways that don't match your attitudes
    D. assist those who are unfamiliar with customs and expectations
    E. do what the group leader tells you to do

98. The Challenger explosion was the result of a problem with the "o rings" that resulted when
    no one in the workgroup challenged the way they were being made. The cause of the
    disaster was ultimately ascribed to _____.
    A. poor engineering
    B. social pressure
    C. groupthink
    D. social norms
    E. conformity

99. Susie and Mitch were voted the best-looking couple in the senior class. They are engaged
    to be married. Their relationship can be explained by the _____.
    A. principle of similarity
    B. principle of proximity
    C. principle of attractiveness
    D. matching hypothesis
    E. attraction hypothesis

100. Milgram's research on obedience was inspired in part by _____.
    A. the animal research of the behaviorists in the 1930s
    B. a need to understand the rise of Hitler in early twentieth-century Europe
    C. the general tendency of 1950s high school students to be conformists
    D. the spread of Communism in post World War II Europe
    E. his interest in why students listened to the professors

Sample Free Response Questions

Respond to each following question using proper psychological terminology. Remember to define the selected terms and support your answer by referencing the situation posed. You have fifty minutes to answer both questions.

1. Many people are very aware of their physical appearance, especially their weight. The way an individual perceives one's body is called body image. Explain how each of the following terms can be applied to one's weight and/or body image.
    A. schema
    B. hypothalamus
    C. modeling
    D. representative heuristic
    E. set point

2. Attending school can facilitate much growth or present challenges for children. Explain how each of the following can affect a person's experiences while attending school.
    A. aphasia
    B. top down versus. bottom up processing
    C. attention
    D. positive reinforcement
    E. self-esteem

Answers to Sample Questions

Multiple Choice Questions

1. C is the correct answer. While some psychologists study mental disorders and others study animals, the main goal of psychology is to study behavior and mental processes.

2. B is the correct answer. The cognitive perspective focuses on our thought processes.

3. C is the correct answer. The psychoanalytic perspective focuses on unconscious conflicts in our id.

4. A is the correct answer. His independent variable of interest is the school attended. Gender is not an identified independent variable.

5. E is the correct answer. The dependent or outcome variable is the SAT scores.

6. B is the correct answer. When a researcher goes out of the laboratory to the place where his participants work/play, that is naturalistic observation.

7. B is the correct answer. With a positive correlation, as one score goes up so does the other score.

8. A is the correct answer. Survey research involves having participants complete a questionnaire even though she is collecting the surveys at the mall.

9. D is the correct answer. The operational definition is the researcher's specification of what he means by the variable.

10. A is a correct answer. The hypothesis is the prediction about the relationship between variables in a study.

11. D is the correct answer. The hippocampus is the part of the brain most involved with memory.

12. A is the correct answer. Vision is located primarily in the occipital lobe.

13. C is the correct answer. The parasympathetic nervous system is the part of the system that helps us calm down.

14. D is the correct answer. The somatic and autonomic systems are subdivisions of the peripheral nervous system.

15. E is the correct answer. The amygdala is the part of the brain most involved with emotions.

16. C is the correct answer. The medulla is the part of the brain most involved with functions such as breathing and blood pressure.

17. B is the correct answer. An fMRI gives us the most information about the activity of cells in the brain.

18. D is the correct answer. The sympathetic nervous system is involved in activating our behavior.

19. B is the correct answer. Past experience helps us understand ambiguous stimuli.

20. C is the correct answer. Negative afterimages are explained by the opponent-process theory of color vision.

21. B is the correct answer. The gate-control theory of pain explains how some incoming pain signals can be blocked.

22. D is the correct answer. Depth perception first appears around the age of six months.

23. E is the correct answer. Jeff's perceptual set led him to anticipate the gun firing.

24. A is the correct answer. An absolute threshold is the amount of stimulation necessary for the stimulus (sound) to be detected.

25. C is the correct answer. Proximity leads us to see the two columns since they are closer together.

26. E is the correct answer. Stage 4 is when the deepest sleep occurs.

27. A is the correct answer. Sleepwalking occurs during the deepest part of sleep when the delta waves show.

28. C is the correct answer. Memory enhancement is not one of the recommended uses of hypnosis.

29. D is the correct answer. With a variable interval, the time interval between rewards varies.

30. B is the correct answer. When you receive the soda from the vending machine, you are being rewarded—operant conditioning.

31. D is the correct answer. Spontaneous recovery is the reappearance of an extinguished conditioned response.

32. C is the correct answer. He has negatively reinforced you. He withdraws the aversive stimulus (the tantrum) when you repeat the behavior he wants (giving in to his demands).

33. B is the correct answer. A cognitive map is a visual representation of a space.

34. A is the correct answer. You have learned what not to do vicariously, a form of social learning.

35. B is the correct answer. Learning involves the strengthening of the synapses of nerve cells.

36. D is the correct answer. The dolphin has become associated with fainting and is a conditioned stimulus.

37. D is the correct answer. Eidetic memory is memory that occurs in images.

38. D is the correct answer. Working memory is the component that processes stimuli.

39. B is the correct answer. In maintenance rehearsal you repeat something in order to better remember it.

40. C is the correct answer. Encoding specificity refers to the idea that memory is encoded using specific cues. Retrieval cues must match the storage cues for easy recall.

41. D is the correct answer. A prototype is the most representative example of a concept.

42. D is the correct answer. The subgoal strategy of problem solving involves breaking a large project into smaller steps.

43. D is the correct answer. A mental set is the tendency to try to solve new problems using old methods.

44. E is the correct answer. Hindsight bias is basing your opinions on an already completed event.

45. C is the correct answer. The normal distribution assumes that a characteristic is spread out evenly through the population.

46. C is the correct answer. Heritability is the amount of trait variation within a group.

47. A is the correct answer. The James-Lange theory of emotions says that we have a physical response (crying) that produces an emotion (sad).

48. B is the correct answer. Thirst is a drive which we are trying to reduce by drinking the Gatorade.

49. D is the correct answer. An internal locus of control means we attribute behavior to our own actions.

50. A is the correct answer. A hassle is a minor annoyance.

51. B is the correct answer. The thalamus is the relay station in the brain that sends messages to the rest of the body.

52. D is the correct answer. The alarm stage is the first stage of the GAS when general arousal occurs.

53. A is the correct answer. The autonomic nervous system activates when we experience fear.

54. A is the correct answer. Reproduction is the biological reason for sex.

55. B is the correct answer. Movement first is detected in the sixteenth week of development.

56. E is the correct answer. According to Ainsworth's research, attachment problems can be overcome although it takes intervention and work.

57. A is the correct answer. Conservation is the understanding that the physical properties of an object do not change if something is added or subtracted.

58. D is the correct answer. Temperament is our inborn disposition.

59. B is the correct answer. In authoritative parenting the child is allowed to make decisions and consequences are related to the child's maturity level.

60. A is the correct answer. Designing an experiment requires abstract thought, characteristic of adolescents in the formal operational stage of cognitive development.

61. A is the correct answer. In stage 1, we think in terms of rewards and punishments.

62. B is the correct answer. In late adulthood, ego-integrity (a sense of wholeness) is challenged by despair (a feeling of disappointment).

63. D is the correct answer. Most psychologists look at behavior as the result of the interaction of nature (genes) and nurture (environment).

64. B is the correct answer. The defense mechanisms operate at the preconscious level.

65. D is the correct answer. Rationalization is the defense mechanism in which we give socially acceptable reasons for actions that are unacceptable to us.

66. C is the correct answer. Bandura proposed a theory of social learning in which we learn vicariously by watching others.

67. B is the correct answer. With an internal locus of control we believe we control our behavior and its outcomes.

68. C is the correct answer. The social cognitive theories of personality are limited in their applicability because they are not comprehensive.

69. D is the correct answer. A good test will have reliability which means that you will get the same results each time you take it.

70. C is the correct answer. Mischel said the situation is most important in determining our personality traits.

71. E is the correct answer. Binet first developed the IQ test to identify students who needed extra help or remediation.

72. E is the correct answer. Fluid intelligence is the ability to see complex relationships and solve complex problems.

73. A is the correct answer. The formula for IQ is mental age divided by chronological age multiplied by 100 ($10/8 \times 100 - 1.25 \times 100$ or 125).

74. D is the correct answer. Howard Gardner's theory of multiple intelligences posits at least nine types of intelligence.

75. C is the correct answer. Social class is not related to parenting skill.

76. C is the correct answer. Recent research suggests that the limbic system is implicated in the development of panic disorder.

77. E is the correct answer. A recent study by NIMH suggests that 15 percent of the population suffers from diagnosable mental disorders.

78. D is the correct answer. A behaviorist believes the reward system in the environment explains behavior.

79. A is the correct answer. Prolonged anxiety or unease is identified as the indicator of distress.

80. C is the correct answer. Somatoform disorders focus on issues of health and bodily symptoms.

81. B is the correct answer. Seasonal affective disorder is a particular form of depression related to a lack of sunlight.

82. D is the correct answer. Recent research has implicated deficiencies in glutamate in the development of schizophrenia.

83. A is the correct answer. Autistic children lack a theory of mind.

84. A is the correct answer. Marilyn Monroe exhibited many symptoms of borderline personality disorder where a person is unstable and given to impulsive behavior.

85. D is the correct answer. A psychiatrist is a medical doctor who can prescribe medication. Under most circumstances, a psychologist cannot prescribe medication.

86. A is the correct answer. While the insight therapies use many theoretical methods, they all encourage the client to understand the difficulties underlying the problem.

87. A is the correct answer. RET is the cognitive-behavioral therapy of Albert Ellis in which the client deals with the self-defeating "shoulds" and "oughts."

88. B is the correct answer. In the client-centered therapy of Carl Rogers, reflective listening is a key technique.

89. C is the answer. This movement seeks to move patients from mental hospitals to community-based treatment.

90. C is the correct answer. Watching a movie of a feared item is used in behavioral therapy and is called symbolic modeling.

91. B is the correct answer. The drugs for treating depression work with the reuptake of neurotransmitters.

92. C is the correct answer. The neo-Freudians emphasize the role of social needs and interpersonal relationships as opposed to the Freudian emphasis on sexual and aggressive desires.

93. D is the correct answer. This study demonstrated the power of the situation to influence behavior.

94. C is the correct answer. Intent is a component of aggression.

95. E is the correct answer. Norms are the unwritten rules for behavior in a particular setting.

96. C is the correct answer. Recent studies show that you increase your chance of getting help if you ask for it.

97. A is the correct answer. Conformity involves changing your attitude and behavior so it matches that of others around you.

98. D is the correct answer. Groupthink occurs when individual members go along with the group and fail to challenge the decision making of the group.

99. D is the correct answer. The matching hypothesis says we find a mate of the same perceived level of attractiveness.

100. B is the correct answer. His research was inspired by his quest to understand how people could blindly follow the Nazis and commit such atrocities.

Suggested Answers to Free Response

These questions will be scored using a rubric.
Terms are worth one point each and applications are worth one point each. The following points should be included in each essay.

Free Response #1

1) Schema is the basic ideas about people, objects, and events based on experiences and stored in long-term memory.
2) If a person was heavy when he was young and he was always teased because of his weight, then his schema of how he looks is as very large. He may have a poor body image.

3) The hypothalamus is the part of the brain that controls hunger.
4) If there is damage to the hypothalamus, weight fluctuation could occur.

5) Modeling is the process of watching and imitating a behavior.
6) If a child models the eating habits of a parent, he may gain weight. If the parents complain about how they look, he may perceive his body image inaccurately.

7) The representative heuristic is a cognitive strategy that focuses on prototypes.
8) If a person sees a celebrity of unhealthy weight as the standard of beauty, then the person may believe that all beautiful people have this body type and this could influence one's body image.

9) Set point is a predetermined natural body weight at which there is little natural deviation.
10) If one's set point is perceived as too high or too low, it could impact body image

Free Response # 2

1) Aphasia is the inability to understand or express language.
2) It is very difficult for someone with aphasia to process speech and language tasks. Thus they may have difficulties in school.

3) Top down processing is concept driven and depends on previous knowledge and expectations. Bottom-up processing creates perceptions from sensory experiences.
4) When students must find an example of a concept, a student uses top down processing. If a student is asked to label an item, the student uses bottom up processing.

5) Attention allows us to select from among many incoming stimuli.
6) Attention to tasks allows the student to focus on the necessary work and not become distracted by other stimuli.

7) Positive reinforcement increases the likelihood that a behavior will be repeated because the behavior receives a reward.

8) When teachers use positive reinforcement, student behavior becomes more cooperative and students achieve greater success.

9) Self-esteem is the part of our self-concept in which we evaluate ourselves.

10) Student self-esteem can influence student achievement.